Foreword

This year, the Y
competition prouc
best poetic talent
and-coming writer

CW01095533

Young Writers v
promote the reading and writing of poetry
schools and to the youth of today. Our books
nurture and inspire confidence in the ability of
young writers and provide a snapshot of poems
written in schools and at home by budding
poets of the future.

The thought, effort, imagination and hard work
put into each poem impressed us all and the
task of selecting poems was a difficult but
nevertheless enjoyable experience.

We hope you are as pleased as we are with the
final selection and that you and your family
continue to be entertained with *Great Minds
From Eastern England Vol II* for many years to
come.

Contents

Michelle Cory (13)	26
Daniyal Khurram (12)	27
Thomas Mills (14)	27
Stacie Ryan (13)	28
Lauren Cowley (13)	28
Sammy Tidd (13)	29
Kurtis Wright (13)	29
Sarah Blyth (14)	30
Ben Sayer (13)	30
Penny Woodcraft (12)	31
Luke Carr (13)	31
Stacey Mann (14)	32
Sara Blade (15)	32
Amber Marjoram (13)	33
Leanne Stubbings (15)	33
Sophie Jay (14)	34
Samantha Orford (14)	34
Robyn Kindred (15)	35
Rommel Worthington (14)	35
Carly Eggett (15)	36
Sarah Green (13)	37
Matthew Fairweather (16)	38
Naomi Gee (14)	38
Kirsty Batterbee (13)	39
Emma Arthur (14)	39
Bilal Khurram (14)	40
Victoria Finlayson (15)	40
Sherri Folkard (13)	41
Leeroi Smith (13)	42
Lee Hansell (15)	42
Judith Muusha (13)	43
John Gaughran (14)	43
Charlotte Cunningham (13)	44
Lucy Payne (14)	45
Jordan Allman (14)	45
Darren Storey (14)	46
Sara-Louise Campbell (15)	46
Cullen Simmons (12)	47
Chelsea Walker	47
Liam Wilder (14)	48
Aaron Clayton Marche (14)	49
Blue Clarke (14)	50

Larissa Warnes (14)   50
Dean Potter (13)   51
Lee Curtis (14)   51
Natalie Gabriel (15)   52
Chris Belas (14)   52
William Knox-Kenike (14)   53
Jessica Tuttle (13)   53
Jason Ramsbottom (12)   54
Wayne Parker (13)   54
Poppy Taylor (14)   55
Ben Affleck (14)   55
Aaron Curran (14)   56
Kirk Sexton (15)   56
Jemma Marjoram (14)   57
Shaun Talbot (15)   57
Nathan Moore (14)   58
Steven Guy (14)   58
Loveness Muusha (13)   59
Amber Waller (14)   59
Jade Stanton (14)   60
Abie Wilson (15)   61
Nicole Reynolds (13)   61
Chris Baker (13)   62
Ashley Lee (14)   62
Stephanie Bullock (15)   63
Daniel Smith (12)   63
Daniel Frazer (12)   64

Great Cornard Middle School, Sudbury
Jessica Broad (13)   64
Corrinne Gallop (12)   65

Great Cornard Upper School, Sudbury
Kit Buchanan (13)   66
Katie Belsey (14)   67
Rebecca Bulmer (14)   68
Rosie Folan (14)   69
Emma King (14)   70
Harriet Livermore (13)   71

Hartismere High School, Eye

Simon Manning (12)	71
Rachel Norburn (12)	72
Callum Towler (13)	72
Jacob Attenborrow (14)	73
Jo Rodgers (13)	73
Amy Stacey (13)	74
Grace Hughes (12)	74
Emma Ellis (13)	75
Jocelyn Berry (13)	76
Abbie Fulcher (13)	77
Livvy Mackay (12)	77
Joshua Bell-Tye (12)	78
Ryan Hill (13)	79
Ben Luckett (13)	79
Alex Frost (12)	80
Emily Millican (13)	80
Simone Braybrook (13)	80
Daniel Rice (12)	81
Sarah Strandoo (13)	81
Rebecca Pizzey (12)	81
Jake Field (12)	82
Cindy Lai (13)	82
Jack Buckmaster (13)	82

Holy Cross Convent School, Chalfont St Peter

Laura Bowler (12)	83
Amy Swallow (13)	83
Lauren Fessey (13)	84
Caitlin Wagstaff (13)	84
Henna A Sachdev (13)	85
Alex Smith (13)	85
Helen Mulhall (13)	86
Frances Bate (12)	87

John Colet School, Wendover

Hannah Curtis (12)	87

Oriel High School, Great Yarmouth

Danielle Smith (14)   88

Riverside Middle School, Bury St Edmunds

Kyle Glennon (11)   88
Shane Carter (11)   89
Amber McLaren (11)   89
Jodie Newton (11)   90
Christopher Willis (11)   90
Jason Sperrink (11)   90

St Bernard's High School, Westcliff-on-Sea

Natacha Killin (17)   91
Rebecca D'Souza (17)   92

St Clement Danes School, Chorleywood

Alice McParlane (13)   92
Elliott Day (13)   93
Oscar O'Mara (13)   93
Fenton Tinkler (13)   94
Matt Hinge (13)   94
Colin Spooner (12)   95
Ross Kershaw (13)   96
Lizzy Eames (13)   96
Lucy Rose McIntosh (13)   97
Nina Boniface (13)   97
Alun Jones (13)   98
Charlotte O'Reilly (13)   99
Tom Hewitt (13)   99
David Grant (13)   100
Charlotte Bodley (13)   100
Alice Denyer (13)   101
Holly Fitch (13)   102
Douglas McAteer (13)   102
Alexandra Shapland (13)   103
Carrie Udall (13)   104
Samantha Blake (13)   105
Gemma Holloway (13)   106
Ed Houghton (13)   107

St John Fisher RC School, Peterborough

Sean Walden (12)	107
Antonio De Miranda (12)	108
Joseph Coombe-Boxall (13)	108
David Tyrrell (13)	109
Ceri Mattless (13)	109
James Chapman (13)	110
Nick Webb (13)	110
Marlerne Smith Star (13)	111
Fezan Akhtar (13)	111
Hannah Bolton (13)	112
Leigh-Anne Dodds (13)	112
Fazeela Akram (13)	113
Tony Baldo (12)	113
Thomas Harwin (13)	114
Natasha Butler (12)	114
Joseph Hostead (13)	115
Michael Wiles (12)	115
Daniel O'Connell (12)	116
Flora Chiutsi (12)	116
Matthew Weston (13)	117
Georgia Farrimond (13)	117
Mariana Mancellos (13)	118
Steven Fairbrace (12)	118
Katie King (12)	118
Johnson Platinum (13)	119
Jessica Guy (12)	119
Chloë Foster (13)	120
Ella Foreman (12)	120
Charlotte Whitwood (11)	121
Esther Beard (12)	121
Ciaran Hyland (12)	122
Sacha Said (13)	122
Christopher White (13)	123
Nick M Webb (13)	123
Sam Stanford (13)	124
Stefan Salerno (12)	124
Hannah Johnson (12)	125
Chantelle Woodbine-Bogle (12)	125
Abdullah Bhatti (13)	126
Ballal Seddique (13)	126

Sawston Village College, Sawston

The Poems

Valentine Pastiche

(Inspired by 'Valentine' by Carol Ann Duffy)

Not a first kiss or a diamond necklace.

I give you a song.
It is the rhythm of my heart on paper.
It sounds heavenly
Like the words you speak.

There.
Its high-pitch notes may burst your ears
Like a scream.
It could bore you completely
Like a hug held too long.

I'm really being truthful.

Not comfort nor relief.

I give you a song.
Its fast diminuendos will worry you,
Harsh and truthful,
As that is
How love is and shall be.

Have it.
Enjoy its uplifting crescendos
While you can.
Quiet.
Its fading shall remind you forever
Of the fading of love.

Rebecca Dell (14)

To Have Life Is To Have Lived

Life!
Replace the F with a V and you get live.
Live, don't lounge.
Live life to the fullest.
Make sure every minute is lived to your destiny.

Don't rush!
When rushing you can't see the little things that make life.

A second in a minute.
A second in an hour and a day.
A second in a year, a decade or century.

You have all the time in the world.
Do what you want to do
And live your own life!

Natasha Green (15)

Untitled

Brightlingsea is a place of fun,
Really, all the children love it,
It has a good seaside too,
Get your ice cream with a side helping of fun,
Had all the fun you can take?
Go to Colchester for more,
Take your children to Brightlingsea,
Love it or hate it,
I know that you will
Never leave,
Goodbye for now,
See you soon,
Enjoy yourself,
And come down to Brightlingsea.

Guy Bryan (12)

One Night

It was a dark, black night,
I was searching for some light,
I got a terrible fright,
I heard a twig break,
And then I looked into the distance and saw a little building,
I saw it was fake,
My heart was pounding,
Everything started surrounding me,
I just wanted to get home,
I had forgotten my phone,
So I couldn't ring my dad,
I was so sad,
I thought I was going to die,
I started to cry,
I looked up into the sky,
I said, 'I just wish I could fly.'

Sean Ewen (14)

Drugs Poem

It makes you weird
It makes you wack
It's very obvious
When you're on crack
Sniff it, smoke it
Stuff it in a bong
Some people do coke
All day long
LSD, LSD
Jump off a bridge
Weee! I can fly
Look at me
If you take ecstasy
The cops will find out
When you pee
All these drugs are used by fools
Using pills 'n' needles 'n' other tools
You might think it's just a bit of fun
But if you take too much you could be done
To do drugs is incredibly stupid
So here's a tip, *just don't do it!*

Sarah Robinson (14)
Ashlyns School, Berkhamsted

War

Sometimes we sit . . . and wait,
Waiting for hours like live bait.
Sometimes we sit and wonder why,
Why are we here and will we die?

Sometimes we see men lying there,
Eyes wide open, a helpless stare.
Sometimes we go over the top,
Watching the pain as men get shot.

Sometimes we crawl on hands and knees,
Thinking all the time of our families.
When will we see them?
Will it be soon?
They would be devastated,
If they saw my tomb.

Sometimes gas, so poisonous,
Floats on by, killing many of us.
'God save us,' we hear men groan,
As they are faced with death alone.

Charlotte White (15)
Ashlyns School, Berkhamsted

My Spirit; Let It Rest

My spirit; let it rest,
Drift away into its nest,
All bruised and torn,
As they begin to mourn.

The puncturing of my skin,
My body; weak and thin.

The growing pain,
Slowly drove me insane,
I couldn't take it any longer,
I wasn't getting any stronger.

The tears from my bruised eyes,
As I write down my goodbyes.

The words they yelled at me,
Why can they not let me be?
I want to be free,
If only they could see.

The rope around my neck in place,
Paleness of my skin and face.

I hide, they seek,
Does nobody hear me shriek?
I collapse to the floor,
They have won this war.

As I take my final leap,
Into my twilight sleep.

My spirit; let it rest,
Drift away into its nest,
All bruised and torn,
As they begin to mourn.

My spirit; it's free now.

Emma Walls (14)
Ashlyns School, Berkhamsted

Nothing Left

The threatening earthquake,
Under the sea,
Shook all around,
The ground trembled,
Demolishing everything
In its path.
Stamping on all
The buildings,
Crushing everything,
Houses, homes flat.
Squeezing the life
Out of everyone.
Exterminating
On the beaches.
The tidal waves
Strangling the locals.
The force of the water
Fighting through walls,
Shredding belongings,
Children losing parents.
Waves chasing the breath
Of terrified citizens.
The waves so perilous
And vigorous,
Annihilating, everything
Gone, nothing left.
The jaws snapping,
Dominating and
Dissecting the tourists;
Nothing left but chaos.

Leanne Ward (11)
Chalkstone Middle School, Haverhill

Everything Gone

The threatening and fierce earthquake
Shook the waves
They threw themselves at houses and hotels
Demolishing the villages
Exterminating sunbeds
Punching through the rocks
The devastating waves crashed through houses
And munched through trees
Slapping the rocks as they rolled
The life-threatening waves drowned the tourists
Families wrestled apart and squeezed to death
Pedestrians demolished and swallowed
Parts of houses and lives gobbled up
Thrown in the water
The breathtaking experience shot down their spines
Houses not strong
Tourists not there
Ground away
And crushed in the water
Screaming and squirming
As people ran for their lives
But the waves pounced on them
Like hungry predators
Dissecting hotels like frogs
Lives snatched
No one, nothing left
Munched away
As the children lost
Their parents
And parents lost their children
Everything crushed.

James Howard (11)
Chalkstone Middle School, Haverhill

Destructive, Heartbreaking Devastation

As the waves gobble the rocks
People scream and run
The waves roll along the villages
Washing trees away
Hurting people
Stealing houses
Demolishing villages
Destructive, heartbreaking devastation
Families torn apart
Searching for their loved ones
People give money to help the survivors
But no one can help the unlucky ones
Laying under the rubble of houses and shops
Lost lives because of this eruption.

Anna Blakeborough (11)
Chalkstone Middle School, Haverhill

Tsunami Hits

With one mighty, powerful punch
It slapped and wrapped itself
Round thousands
Grabbed and shredded all in its way
It swept through hotels and beach huts
To create a huge disaster
It somersaulted and strangled
And tangled victims
Crawled round trees
Swallowed people down
Into the deep, blue sea
Shattered lives forever
Now all that's left is a
Horrendous wreck.

Kiara Larkin (11)
Chalkstone Middle School, Haverhill

Tsunami

It started with a plate movement,
In the Indian Ocean.
No warning at all.
Slowly emerging, it somersaulted
Towards shore,
Demolishing boats,
Fishing was over.
Trampling on people and houses,
A murderer chasing,
Grabbing children.
Pushing this way and that.
Annihilating as it rolled,
Destructively crushing buildings.
Pouncing on houses,
As it punched vehicles,
Swallowing wood and bricks.
It gobbled hotels,
And strode through cafes.
Watching people weep,
Screaming for help.
It threw houses and vehicles
At the people behind.
It started to slow and die.
It left destruction,
It was like a signature,
Leaving 150,000 dead.

Ben Perrett (11)
Chalkstone Middle School, Haverhill

The Tsunami

An almighty wave zoomed across the sea
Came into shore and swallowed everything in its path
Frightening, as it surrounded people
So dramatic, as it emerged from nowhere
It strangled houses, squashed vehicles and murdered
It left over 150,000 people dead
Hundreds of people injured
And thousands of people still missing
Loved ones lost forever
Survivors, crying out for food and water
Children screaming for their parents
People with diseases
No hospitals to send them to
No doctors to give advice
No medicine to cure them
People are homeless
Have nowhere to sleep
Living alone
Children can't sleep without a bedtime story
Bedtime hug
Bedtime kiss
Devastation is all around
As a beautiful holiday resort
Is turned into a haunting ghost town.

Chloe Savory (11)
Chalkstone Middle School, Haverhill

Tragedy

The wave rose high,
Snatching the trees and cars,
Destroying whatever was in its way,
Cars and buses, houses and trees,
A never-ending tragedy.
The wave swallowed villages,
Tourists swept by the powerful beast,
Floating around, hoping they would be found,
The angry wave gobbled,
Devouring schools, children, adults,
A never-ending tragedy.
Screaming, tourists shouting,
They wait and wait but nothing,
People found more missing,
Others safe, others lost,
Families devastated, traumatised,
But still the waves annihilate, exterminate,
Is there no end to this angry beast?
At last the beast disappears,
People found dying, injured,
Buildings destroyed, homes crashed,
Hotels smashed, shops gone.
This never-ending tragedy.

Aggrey Wanjala (11)
Chalkstone Middle School, Haverhill

The Tsunami

It was a peaceful and pretty place
When under the sea
Two plates moved
First the earthquake, next the murderous wave
That thundered and crashed
Through the town
It toppled cars and ripped up houses
It was a dramatic but deadly scene
So monstrous and strong
The wave bundled through villages
On its journey it gobbled up people
And pounced on houses, breaking in
And shouting, 'It's time to die!'
As it punched the family and snatched them away
It snapped trees, crushed houses
And that was the end.

Lauren Chilcott (11)
Chalkstone Middle School, Haverhill

The River

The river is calm like a cat waiting to be awakened . . .
By a crashing and bashing and smashing waterfall.
The river is rushing like a volcano waiting to explode . . .
By a call from the singing and shimmering, beautiful river.
Splishing and splashing and sploshing,
Washing and wishing and whistling on the rocks.
The river is charging and barging
Like a rhino, chasing the rapids which are
Thumping and bumping and jumping,
Curling and whirling and twirling over the rocks,
Sprinting really fast, like a race to the sea,
Which is where it will end its massive journey.

Alex Nagy (11)
Chalkstone Middle School, Haverhill

Tsunami

The harsh wind roared
As the pedestrians' screams filled the villages,
Nobody was warned of the terrible tsunami.

The tsunami snatched the lives of millions;
It grabbed the hearts of millions, loved ones lost forever.

Village houses were crushed
By the enormous, fighting tidal wave,
Houses not strong enough for the powerful blast of water.

Delirious some, waking to this traumatising,
Murderous wave of terror,
Some lucky on high land,
Some not so lucky as they were swallowed whole
By this mass mutilator.

Exterminating more people by the second,
The tidal wave pounced,
Some ran but couldn't get away from the catastrophic tsunami.
Tourists, some dead; villagers, many more dead,
Missing people, still not found, families are torn apart.

Rebecca Hawker (10)
Chalkstone Middle School, Haverhill

Devastation Awakening

As the powerful, horrific
Waves slapped the cliffs
Afterwards somersaulting
Back into the ocean
Murdering, strangling
Swallowing, snatching
Crushing
Still vicious and powerful
It carried on
Traumatising people
Their lives once carefree
These sickening, life-threatening
Waves, so horrendous
Killing and
Demolishing villages
Heartbreaking, lost loved ones
People giving money to save
The lucky ones
Whose lives were spared
In this unforgettable earthquake.

Victoria Sparrow (11)
Chalkstone Middle School, Haverhill

The Murderous Wave

Discs rubbed
Earthquake shook
Tsunami came
Crushed people
Gobbled trees
Flattened houses
Trampled all it encountered

The immeasurable tsunami
Somersaulted dramatically
As it rolled over hotels
People screamed
Haunting and hideous

The murderous wave
Slapped buildings and punished victims
Bodies emerged out of the water
Bobbing, lifeless

Aid came
Some saved
Many died
Hundreds missing
Villagers left with nothing
Catastrophic damage
Now they start again.

Tim Brown (11)
Chalkstone Middle School, Haverhill

Devastation All Around

It started with an earthquake,
Crash, boom, shake!
The wave somersaulted over the island,
Gobbling everything, demolishing, dissecting.

Snatching people on its way,
Squeezing the life from them.
Rolling through the land,
Swallowing, exterminating.

The tragic tidal wave,
Murdering, munching.
As powerful as a bolt of lightning,
Pouncing, chasing.

The horrendous disaster,
Breaking people's hearts.
Strangling trees,
Drowning their homes.

Devastation all around,
Screaming, weeping.
People trying to escape,
But the wave just kept striding towards them.

Sophie Walker (11)
Chalkstone Middle School, Haverhill

Tsunami

The lethal earthquake
Created the destructive tsunami
Obliterating everything in its path
It was snatching and slapping
Like an indestructible monster
Washing away homes

It somersaulted over the islands
And strangled the trees
Swallowed the leaves
Screaming, screeching
Emerging and chasing
As it punched and pounced

This heartbreaking wave
Trampled and munched
As it rolled and crashed
Whistled and smacked
Demolishing the islands
As it jabbed at the people like a boxer

It was a devastating day
When that disastrous wave
Killed so many
It traumatised and terrorised
As the beautiful islands
Were washed away.

Jake Duffy (11)
Chalkstone Middle School, Haverhill

The Sea Of Death

The fierce wave struck the ground,
Obliterating everything in its path.
Grabbing people,
Rolling them back and forth.
The deadly tidal wave,
Swallowing all their lives.
The violent wave,
Dissecting, demolishing,
Attacking and mutilating.
The horror people felt that day,
Dramatically finding the bodies
Of their loved ones . . .
The nations' donations
Will help to save lives.

Shannon Farnham (11)
Chalkstone Middle School, Haverhill

Disaster Strikes

The ground wobbles, cracks and slaps
Horrendous smacks hit the ground
The sea snatches and bashes all in its path
Everything slides and collides
Fatal screams under and under
Cannot be heard by a bird
Demolishing waves that curl and whirl
Dancing and prancing through the land
Swaying and praying through the village
Crunching and munching through trees
Bang, crash! Again and again
Floating and bloating, through it goes
Children alone, people alone
It goes alone.

Tom Jury (11)
Chalkstone Middle School, Haverhill

Devastating Waters

The wave arose
The land was crushed
Everything was gone
People dead
People strangled
By the hungry wave
It smashed the rocks

The wave arose
The land was crushed
Everything was gone
People scared
Water everywhere
People injured
Villages trampled
Disaster here
Disaster there
Fear is everywhere.

Josh Firman (11)
Chalkstone Middle School, Haverhill

So Ignorant

The unforeseen wave slapped the land,
Terrified people ran away,
Brute force knocked down buildings,
Heartbroken children screamed,
Colossal features washed clean down,
Vast noises could be heard,
Throwing bricks everywhere,
A violent current sweeping,
Not only one wave though,
But two murderous waves,
Sharp things a-floating,
So ignorant, no care,
Running the streets,
Looking for a new target,
Villagers left devastated,
The lethal wave thundered through towns,
A catastrophe causing irreversible damage.

Luke Youngs (11)
Chalkstone Middle School, Haverhill

Wave Devastation

Happy people smiling, carefree
Towns bursting with people
Bang! The earth was shaken
Screaming people falling
Tourists on the beach drowning
A tidal wave
Somersaulting through the town
Strangling as the waves pounced and crushed children
Houses and shops destroyed
Rubble trapping victims, trampled over trees
Journalists traumatised
More and more waves emerged, killer waves
Squeezing out life
Slowly the waves disappeared
Thousands of devastated people
Over 150,000 people dead
Mourning families
Lives never the same again.

Alex Young (11)
Chalkstone Middle School, Haverhill

Tsunami

No early warning
To prepare
People lay on the beaches
In a second they were dead
Helpless cries in the village
The crushing monster is coming
Mother and child cling together
As the wave comes tumbling in
Villages being destroyed in a flash
As the earth shook and the waves trembled
Thousands were dying
Friends, family and tourists all drowned
By the obliterating monster
That we call the sea
And when it was over
And thousands were dead
That's when we started to help
We raised a lot to show we care.

Sophie Backler (11)
Chalkstone Middle School, Haverhill

The Sea

The unchartered sea,
Blue and tranquil,
The sound of waves soothes me,
An icy sheet of blue covers the beach like a blanket,
Enchanted by the rhythmic waves,
Sparkling crystal clear through the days.

Jonathan Abery (12)
Earlham High School, Norwich

However Far

However far I run
However much I hide
I can't get rid of this feeling
That lives deep inside.

I've tried to run away
From the hurt and the pain
But it keeps coming back to me
Over and over again.

Why did you rape me
And leave me like this?
You said it was natural
You gave me your kiss.

You made me feel dirty
Disgusting and bruised
I was only ten
I had been so used.

Five years later
I confessed to a friend
She said it was wrong
She said it was bent.

I cried and cried
Till my tears ran dry
You manipulated me
You had been so sly.

Now I've left
Unsure what to do
Because all of my life
I've been wrecked by you.

Donna Stanley (14)
Earlham High School, Norwich

When I Am Gone

When I am gone, please don't weep
I'll be there to watch you sleep
I have gone to the other side
To be greeted by the loved and lost of my life
Do not fear or cry for long
You must not grieve, I have not gone
I'll be the hand that leads you through
And I'll always be there to watch over you

When I am gone, you must not cry
For now I am safe, I will never leave your side
I shall watch you in whatever life may bring
I will keep you safely tucked under my wing.

Stacie Curtis (15)
Earlham High School, Norwich

The Weather

Sunny, windy, gloomy, rainy
All the weathers we get daily
The polar caps are melting
Cos people don't care about global warming
Hurricanes rip up the ground
Tsunamis flood all the dry land
Landslides invade people's houses
Heat waves burning everything in their path
When are we going to understand
What's happening all around?

Doug Sexton (14)
Earlham High School, Norwich

The Sea

I laid down upon the seashore,
And dreamed of a little space,
I heard the great waves roar and break,
As I watched the lifeblood of the Earth.

My fingers began twitching,
As I played with the little, grey pebbles,
The waves thrashed up, the waves soothed down,
Both thundering and textured.

The salty pebbles, smooth and round,
Were sitting by my side,
Like little people who I had found,
Sitting and bathing on the great sands.

The grains of sand completely tiny,
Ran peacefully through my fingers,
The sparkling sun shone down on me,
With warm, yet restless beams.

I lay on some forgotten shore,
As I lie and play here today,
The tranquillity of the creatures swimming below,
Made me a calming animal.

The waves rocked like a child in arms,
As they flashed like rabbits when they leapt,
The whitish part of their tails on show,
Like playing leapfrog over ships nearby.

As it peacefully brainwashes you into relaxation,
The sea is a wonderful place.

Michelle Cory (13)
Earlham High School, Norwich

The Sea

The sea was dark, the sea was grey,
On the night of a winter's day,
Uncontrollable waves rumbled along the bay,
They were beasts you could not slay.

The fishes swam with an unstoppable urge,
You could jump right in and not stop the surge,
They would swim and swim,
Until the sea and sand would merge.

The moon would drown,
The sun would be crowned,
As it set in the horizon,
The water would turn crimson.

The cliff was the king,
The water would stop reigning,
The sea fought the cliff with splashing,
But the cliff would stand tall and surviving.

The sea will be always mighty,
The sea will never end,
The sea will stay forever,
The sea will be forever,
Neither foe or friend.

Daniyal Khurram (12)
Earlham High School, Norwich

London Bombings

Why bomb London?
Why bomb at all?
Are these people thick
Or just plain sick?
Those innocent people chosen that day
Why kill so many, especially that way?
Why bomb? Why not save?
What is this world turning into?
Why not help turn this hectic world the right way round?

Thomas Mills (14)
Earlham High School, Norwich

The Sea

The sea is sharp, rocky like thunder
Its set of jaws lay beneath its prey.
Now it's time to say goodbye
Swish, swoosh, it's all you hear.
Then all of a sudden the sea calms down
Now it's all tender.

The smell is sweet, the air is cold
And lets the wind unfold.
All I see is the deep blue sea
The seagulls laugh as they flutter by.

The sea is as cold as ice
It's like the jagged rocks along the beach.
The sea is the same colour as your eyes
So in a way it's as though the sea
Watches everyone in every direction.

Stacie Ryan (13)
Earlham High School, Norwich

The Sea

The sea was warm and calm,
Its surface smooth and shiny as lip balm.

The water lapped against the sand,
And the man outstretched his hand.

The tranquillity put him at ease,
As he walked in up to his knees.

The salty blue flood swirled around,
As the fish swam, homeward bound.

He wandered slowly into the sea,
If only he could swim as well as me.

Lauren Cowley (13)
Earlham High School, Norwich

The Sea And Me!

The cool, calm, collective sea,
It runs through the veins, the heart of me.

In night and day,
The sea will stay,
Forever in my heart.

The smell you can tell,
It is the sea,
Forever, forever, forever in me.

In night and day,
The sea will stay,
Forever in my heart.

Forever we shall stay,
Until our dying day,
The sea, the sea and me.

Sammy Tidd (13)
Earlham High School, Norwich

Sea

The cold ocean battered
Against the sandy coastline,
The sea howled like a wolf
As its crystal clear surface
Faded into the night sky.

The villagers on the pier
Are being battered and
Bruised as the unpredictable
Beast of an ocean roars
At their presence.

Kurtis Wright (13)
Earlham High School, Norwich

Mr Sea

The sea chilled my skin to the bones
I hate the sea, the way it shines and acts all distressed.

Wild at night and calm at day.
The deep, cold sea wrapped around my neck
Trying to pull me to the rocks below.

It was sparkling like a star in the dark sky
Moaning like my mum does when I don't tidy up my room.

As it pulled me under the calm waves went wild.
As my heart took its last beat
A shiny light drove down.
As a dirty hand reached out
As men and women screamed out.
And all I could think is,
Why did Mr Sea pick on me?

Sarah Blyth (14)
Earlham High School, Norwich

The Wash

The sea laid peacefully over a bed of thick sand,
As over the horizon hovered a dismal cloud band.

The water rose rapidly and the sea became rough,
The trees started swaying as the wind gave a huff.

The fisherman's boat moored at the quay,
Began to slowly drift away.

The birds fled in horror as darkness arose,
As mammals on land were startled and froze.

Yet this is not the worst to come,
We're in for a shock when the damage is done.

Ben Sayer (13)
Earlham High School, Norwich

Sea Poem

The waves wave to welcome you in
They suck you in like a black hole
Swallowing your soul

The waves, spiky like a prick to your finger
Asleep for 100 years
Stuck in a trance
At first glance
Some people are addicted to drugs
But not me
I am addicted to the sea
I sneak to the shore every night
Just sitting
Just waiting
For the end of the world
Just me and it
Together forever.

Penny Woodcraft (12)
Earlham High School, Norwich

The Sea

The sea is big, quiet and tranquil
With sudden bursts of turbulence and very enchanting waves

It is lonely, blue, sparkling and eternal
And disturbed by a big, metallic ship

It is salty, majestic and silent with
Seagulls disturbing its continuous chanting.

Luke Carr (13)
Earlham High School, Norwich

My Feelings

My feelings are here, there, everywhere
Sometimes I'm up
The next time I'm down
Where do my feelings come from?
My heart, my brain, my tum?
Sometimes I feel upset, tearful and sad
I feel alone in the deep, deep, dark
Where do my feelings go?
Up, up and away

Feelings are weird
They always change
One day you're happy
The next day you're sad
Feelings are different
You get love, friendship feelings as well
Sometimes you're hurt
Your heart's broken in two
But you can live through it
Trust me, I do!

Stacey Mann (14)
Earlham High School, Norwich

The White Moon

From the dark there is the love,
The stars of night shine above.
The white moon is here to stay,
Along the crescent water bay.
You will see I'm here for you,
In your arms forever true.
If you choose to be with me,
Look in your heart and there I'll be.

Sara Blade (15)
Earlham High School, Norwich

Think, Don't Drink . . .

The wind blows on my soft face sending a chill down my spine,
Swiftly the trees swaying side to side,
The dark clouds cover the empty sky.
The sight of the black van getting closer.
The light gleaming out brightening the road up,
Blinking faster and faster.
Noise around me but all I can focus my eyes on
Is this moving van beeping and honking.

My whole life is flashing towards me on the back of this black van
And all I can do is just stand there not moving
It's as if it is waiting for it to happen,
My feet are stuck . . .

Amber Marjoram (13)
Earlham High School, Norwich

My Loss

You are the lost part of my heart
And I will never forget you and the times we shared.
Although you are far away you are still in my dreams.

Every day when I wake up and you are not here,
And when I close my eyes at night you will appear
And gently whisper my name, silently in the wind.

And then you will slowly put me to bed
With your warm touch of love and say goodnight.

Leanne Stubbings (15)
Earlham High School, Norwich

African Children

Can you see them crying?
Can you hear them scream?
For they might never see tomorrow,
You might never hear them sing.

With no money and no food,
With no houses and no clothes.
They lay on the dry ground,
Waiting for a miracle to spring.

Flies are buzzing all around,
Hear the crying, a horrible sound.
How would you feel in their shoes,
Without material things?

So make the right decision, G8,
Do it for the people
Who have nothing to give the world
And who are dying every three seconds.

You can change the world!

Sophie Jay (14)
Earlham High School, Norwich

My Helpful Dog

My helpful dog
Is always by my side,
Wherever I walk, whenever I ride.
On bus or on train,
Whenever I walk, even in rain.
Around the house he is my light.
He guides me up the stairs at night.
By my side he remains until I wake,
At morning break.
My life will never be the same,
It began the day he came.
Guess what my dog is
 . . . Guide dogs are smart.

Samantha Orford (14)
Earlham High School, Norwich

Everyone's Equal

Does it matter about . . .
How people look
Or how they speak?
Everyone's equal.

Does it matter about . . .
The clothes people wear
Or the colour of their hair?
Everyone's equal.

Life is not about being mean
But many people are.
I believe it's because they
Don't know why they're here.

I don't know the purpose of life
But I'm sure it's not to fight.
I ask everyone: Please don't argue because
Everyone's equal.

Robyn Kindred (15)
Earlham High School, Norwich

Snowfall

When the snow falls down
Friends are out to look around
They admire it.

Children are about
All you can hear is laughter
That makes us all smile.

When the snow is gone
Everyone has all gone
All I can hear is cars.

Rommel Worthington (14)
Earlham High School, Norwich

Love

Words cannot describe how I feel for you
And deep down in my heart I know you feel it too
There's a difference between us
This I know
But nothing can stop me from letting my love show
I missed you so much, I saw you in my sleep
And every time I thought of you
My heart began to weep
We're destined to be together and never be apart
And you will always have
A place right in my heart.

Just wanna say I love you
And this will always stand
My heart skips a beat
When you hold my hand
Your heart is made of gold
Your lips as soft as silk
Your scent is like a flower,
A flower that will never wilt.

Your face is like an angel
Your halo's shedding light
Your neck is nice and slender
Your eyes are so bright
You kiss me so tender
That's why I love you!

Carly Eggett (15)
Earlham High School, Norwich

Let Me Be . . .

Let me be your scarf,
Breathing in your smell,
Let me be your other half,
I will treat you really well,
Let me be your shower,
Keeping you nice and clean,
You make the rules,
I wanna be yours.

Let me be your oven,
You will never get cold,
You can count on my loving,
It will never get old,
Let me be your clock,
I won't ever run out,
There is no doubt,
I wanna be yours.

Let me be your sun,
Shining down upon you,
Let me be the one,
To always be around you,
Let me be your pillow,
Holding all your secrets,
I don't wanna be anyone else's,
I just wanna be yours!

Sarah Green (13)
Earlham High School, Norwich

The Incomplete Family

The mums and dads abuse their young children,
With sticks and knives they constantly beat them.
For all the trouble the teenagers cause,
Their parents can never sit down and pause.
Gramps and Granny just sit around all day,
While their mental grandchildren go out to play.
When the police come banging on the door,
For hitting an old lady and knocking her to the floor.
The brat in the house hides under his bed,
Waiting for the psycho dad with the hammerhead.
A blow to the stomach and a shot to the face,
Then burnt to death on the fireplace.
The police return, this time with a coffin,
To collect the body that's been burnt rotten.
The dad goes to jail and the mother can't cope,
So she turns to the drink and she smokes the dope.
I don't want to give the impression
That all families are bad,
Unless you're in my shoes
Where your parents are mad.

Matthew Fairweather (16)
Earlham High School, Norwich

Grandad, You Mean So Much . . .

Grandad, I love you for always being there
You've been my inspiration and showed you always care
We've shared so much laughter
You've always given me praise
So I thank my lucky stars
For all our happy days.

Naomi Gee (14)
Earlham High School, Norwich

In My Head

In it I think of my dog
And also my pet mouse.
I think of going on holiday
And living in a different house.

I think of Coronation Street
Emmerdale and EastEnders too.
I think of all my homework
And how much there is to do.

I think about my family
I think about my friends.
I think about the universe
And when it's gonna end.

I think about the living
I think about the dead.
I think about a lot of things
And that's what's in my head.

Kirsty Batterbee (13)
Earlham High School, Norwich

Up In Heaven

When I go to Heaven
And you're not there

I'll carve your name
In a golden chair

I'll tell the angels
Up above

You're the only one
I ever loved.

Emma Arthur (14)
Earlham High School, Norwich

It's Just Not The Same

When I look at you,
It's just not the same,
You filled me with hate,
To you it's all a game,
You've moved on again,
And left me with this pain,
You didn't extinguish,
But killed the flame,
Like a bad memory,
You speak of my name,
Killing me slowly,
Is all this shame,
You made the mistake,
But I get the blame,
Still thinking of you,
I'm far past insane,
Because when I look at you,
It's just not the same.

Bilal Khurram (14)
Earlham High School, Norwich

He

He's my one and only,
When I'm with him I'm never lonely.
Seeing him every day,
I love him, that's all I can say.

My heart is complete,
No other could compete.
He's definitely the one,
He's my shining sun.

Victoria Finlayson (15)
Earlham High School, Norwich

Let Me Be . . .

Let me be your raincoat
For when it rains all day.
Let me be your suitcase
For when you go away.
Let me be your hair comb
For those frequent bad hair days.
Let me be your stylish car
For when you drive away.

Let me be your radio
You can dance all night to.
Let me be your telephone
So I can talk to you.
Let me be your heater
So I can keep you warm.
Let me be your umbrella
To shelter you from the storm.

Let me be your teddy bear
To cuddle you at night.
Let me be your shining lamp
To keep you from the fright.
Let me be your towel
To keep you warm and dry.
Let me be your tissue
For when you want to cry.

Sherri Folkard (13)
Earlham High School, Norwich

The Fight

Clay comes out to meet Liston
But Liston starts to retreat,
If he backs up any further
He'll end up in a ringside seat,
Clay wings with his left
He swings with his right,
Look at young Cassius carry the fight,
It's just a matter of time before Clay lowers the boom,
It will lift Liston right out of the room.

The referee wears a deepening frown,
He cannot start counting till Sonny comes down,
The crowd goes frantic,
The radio stations have picked him up
And he's somewhere over the Atlantic.

Who would have known when they came to see the fight,
They were going to see the launching of a human satellite?
Who would have known when they put down their money,
They were going to see the total eclipse of the Sonny?

Leeroi Smith (13)
Earlham High School, Norwich

The Lake

The lake is deep,
Shimmers like a sheet of glass
Lapping against the shoreline,
Full with emotion and feeling.

As deep as the Earth,
With emotion, listening to passers-by.
Embracing all feelings that it encounters.
The lake can be vengeful or
Overjoyed, taking lives or saving lives.

Lee Hansell (15)
Earlham High School, Norwich

Love

My love is deeper than your thoughts
I can't sleep without thinking of you, my sweetheart
My dreams are all filled with your loving heart
Your sweet tongue brings out words of joy and happiness

You are like a blooming flower
Bringing in peace and joy
Your love endures forever
My love makes you smile without forgetting me

Without you, my sweetheart, my love is covered in wounds
The sickness is very difficult to heal
When you are beside me my dreams become true
My love lasts forever.

Judith Muusha (13)
Earlham High School, Norwich

The Vampire

As the sun goes down out of our sight
Drowned by the pitch-black darkness and midnight falls
Creatures of the night come and hunt.
Their skin is long dead and white.
Their eyes are crimson-red like what they hunt.
Their fangs are sharp like daggers and perfect for their cause.
They move silent like the wind.
If you see them before it's too late
There is nowhere to run and no shadow to hide.
Fighting is futile for not even the Reaper can claim them.
So when you're alone at night and the darkness calls your name
There is nothing that can be done.

John Gaughran (14)
Earlham High School, Norwich

I Wanna Be Yours

Let me by your teddy bear,
When you need a hug.
Let me be your cup of tea,
In your special mug.
Let me be your raincoat,
For those frequent rainy days.
Let me be your flower,
In the middle of May.
I don't care,
I wanna be yours.

Let me be your wings,
So you can fly away.
Let me be your sun,
On a rainy day.
Let me be your flower,
In a special pot.
Let me be your fire,
To keep you nice and hot.
You call the shots,
I wanna be yours.

Let me be your stars,
To shine at night.
Let me be your mountain,
So you can climb that height.
Let me be your purse,
If you like your money.
Let me be your wild bear,
To eat your honey.
I don't want to be hers,
I wanna be yours.

Charlotte Cunningham (13)
Earlham High School, Norwich

Summer Holidays

Summer holidays
They are so great
I can stay out
Till half-past eight

Sun hat on
Suncream out
All I want to do
Is give a big shout

No homework
No school
All we have to do
Is jump in a pool

Now it's all over
and back to work
Worksheets and maths
School is such hard work.

Lucy Payne (14)
Earlham High School, Norwich

Mum

You have always been there
Through all of my bad times
Through thick and thin
You've warmed my skin
It's obvious you care.

And I may not always show it
But you shine as brightly as the sun
You might not even believe me
But I love you dearly, Mum!

Jordan Allman (14)
Earlham High School, Norwich

Fire

The blazing, crackling, cold blue flames
Ascending to the heavens.
Burning and soothing, gently gripping the knife
And stabbing its victims' backs as they flee.
The ends of the flames licking the clouds
And soaring above the birds.
The red-hot heat of the fire
Flickering like a dying light bulb.

Its powerful arms reaching out to the heavens above.
Then suddenly its dying limbs fading down to the hells beneath.
Powerful and dangerous, dancing below the moonlight.
But gentle and subtle in the water of its surroundings.
Beauty in the right hands but terror to the evil eyes.
Always omniscient in the darkness of the clouds.

Darren Storey (14)
Earlham High School, Norwich

My Star

I see your tears roll down and fall
You've never missed a single ball
Each night you cry a lonely tear
Each consumed by living fear
You are the one I do love
My sweet, lonely, heartfelt dove
I love you now, I love you more
The love we have was here before
You are the star in my eye
You're like the sun in the sky
Seeing you has brought me here
Time has come, I will be near.

Sara-Louise Campbell (15)
Earlham High School, Norwich

The Monster

It lashes out every few seconds,
You hear it in the wind as it whistles and beckons.
It is rough, it is bad,
If it gets you it will drive you mad.
It is immeasurable,
It is never leisurable.
It will get you, it will, it will,
This sub-aquatic monster will kill.

It is grotty, hopeless, unbound,
If you look carefully it's all around.
You don't know what I'm talking about?
I'll give you a clue.
It is big, salty and blue.
Yes, well done, it's the sea,
This is a poem made by me.

Cullen Simmons (12)
Earlham High School, Norwich

My Mate Josh

My mate Josh is so annoying
He sits in lessons and does his drawings
My mate Josh smokes and smokes
He's turning into a very big dope.

My mate Josh always talks
He never runs, always walks
My mate Josh likes to sing
He always goes *ding-ding-ding*.

My mate Josh is very naughty
He likes the film 'Get Shorty'
My mate Josh is a girl
He always dances, spins and twirls.

Chelsea Walker
Earlham High School, Norwich

War In Iraq

The war in Iraq is happening every day,
When British and Americans work together,
Not letting them have their say.
Let's call in an air strike or charge in all guns blazing,
The sun is hot but there is no time for lazing.

It must be hard for both teams, one bullet is all it will take,
This is a real war, it is not a fake.
Thousands of men die each day, changing everyone's lives,
Bees buzzing from their beehives.

Terrorists hiding in buildings or underground,
Hearing big bangs or a loud sound.
They do not give up without a fight,
Do not want to be caught in an enemy's sight.

When each day ends another begins in a blink of an eye,
I see men lying and left to die.
It is scary pulling a trigger,
The noise of a gun sounds like a digger.

Hearing the noise of a jumpjet roar,
My arms are getting sore.
As I hear the noise of a tank,
If it is not an ally we should suppress the flank.
If we capture their leader it is all over,
This part of the battlefield is full of clover.
If we hold on and defend,
In this war we will win and that will be the end.

Liam Wilder (14)
Earlham High School, Norwich

The World

What's wrong with the world that we live in?
People keep on giving in.
The roads are getting faster and faster,
The world is just a total disaster.

George Bush sitting there talking b******t,
Because he walks about thinking he's all it.
Bush sits there eating a large muffin,
When there's Africa with absolutely nothin'.

Why do we have to cope with the world out there?
People laying in fear.
You can't just relax on a beach picking pebbles,
All you see is lots and lots of rebels.

Sitting there having an ice-cold beer,
Really, does anyone care?
People walking with a huge, big frown,
Bombs dropping down.

Listen out the window, what can you hear?
All I can hear is a big, big fair,
The world is just so bad,
One word for it is sad.
Why can't you walk by the lake and watch a deer?
The only one that can change it is the one up there.

Aaron Clayton Marche (14)
Earlham High School, Norwich

Sea Britain

Britain's sea sparkles like a star
And shines like the sun,
It is as calm as a tree
But stings like a bee.
Sometimes drowns the people around
But when alone it doesn't make a sound.
The kids play during the day
But it will always be there for another day.
The sea is wild
And acts like a child.
The sea is quiet
But it will not deny it.
The sea has a mind
A mind of its own
But has a mind of a 9-year-old.
The sea reminds me of quicksand
Because when you're on it you'll keep going down
And there's no one to pull you out.
You keep on falling
And no one can hear you calling
So you end up self-destructing.

Blue Clarke (14)
Earlham High School, Norwich

My Cousin

There once was a little girl
She was my little cousin
She was all so cute
When she was born
But now she is one she is a pain
We now have a new addition
And she is little Isobel

Ella and Isobel are the best cousins I have ever had.

Larissa Warnes (14)
Earlham High School, Norwich

London 2012

London 2012 was announced on the 6th,
The best day of the year for the people of London.

As work starts to begin
The cheering echoes through the cities of Great Britain.
Hugs and tears still going with the celebration of 2012.

Our country hosts the greatest stage of the year,
The best players in the world
And we can even become athletes one day
Competing for the great country we live in.

People shouting everywhere,
'2012, 2012!'

Dean Potter (13)
Earlham High School, Norwich

Chelsea

Chelsea, Chelsea, Chelsea, they are the best team,
Forget Liverpool, Man U, Arsenal, just remember that team.

The team that won the Premiership by miles are that great team.
The team with pride and confidence,
The team that shows them up.

The Blues with dignity are the ones to win
So step back, Steven Gerrard, we don't need you here to sing.

I am proud of Chelsea, all the matches they've won.
So get down on your knees, you Liverpool scum.

Lee Curtis (14)
Earlham High School, Norwich

Grandad

(In loving memory of my grandad Alex)

Grandad, I know you can see in Heaven
At least I hope you can,
My life is not the same without you here,
I am here, just here by myself
And I don't like it much.
I wish things could go back to the way they were.
Grandad, I am only 15
And I probably don't know much
But I know you died and that's what I don't like much.
Nothing is the same anymore,
I feel like I am here without anyone to talk to,
Grandma is the same,
I wish she was though,
She really misses you.
Grandad, can you try to come back?

Natalie Gabriel (15)
Earlham High School, Norwich

London 2012

The city withholds the world's most talented athletes.
The athletes stream along the track at their fastest.
The stadium is a gigantic beehive.
The London tube slithers around London non-stop.
The super Brit Kelly Holmes succeeds in winning a fabulous gold.
The Japanese without a gold walking away bold.
They have been told.
We are British, proud and are a stronghold.

Chris Belas (14)
Earlham High School, Norwich

Homelessness

I have no home
I'm so alone
With no roof over my head
A cold pavement as my bed

Every night I get so cold
All my food is covered in mould
I've got no one to love or hold
I'm alone as I slowly grow old

Imagine all those lucky people
Roast dinners, cold tarts with treacle
They have a family to love and hold
As I sit here cold

Homelessness is no life to live
Not for an adult or for a kid
So be grateful for what you have got
If not you will lose the lot.

William Knox-Kenike (14)
Earlham High School, Norwich

The Shiny Sea!

It can be calm or loud when it's deep and cold.
Maybe it can be clear or dirty or maybe salty and smelly.
Sometimes wild, sometimes not.
It can be blue or green as well as aggressive or lonely.
Sometimes choppy, maybe distressed.
It does not matter what it's like
Because people play in the loud, choppy, aggressive, dirty
And shiny, cold sea.
The sea can be as cold as winter
And not hot in summer.
So whatever the weather or the season
It's going to be cold and maybe loud.

Jessica Tuttle (13)
Earlham High School, Norwich

The Sea

The sea is rough, the sea is calm,
And is as soft as a baby's palm,
It can be stormy and bleak,
And it's bad in a boat to have a leak.

The sea is as blue as can be,
It is as bright as a bumblebee,
The sea is full of lots of waves,
And under the water there could be caves.

The sea is big, the sea is deep,
And when you jump in you take a leap,
The sea is tranquil and also soothing,
Yet the sea is always moving.

The sea is filled with lots of fish,
And some are caught and put on a dish,
The sea is turbulent like a jumbo jet,
And in the sea people look for a fishy pet.

The poem is now at an end,
And just remember, the sea's your friend.

Jason Ramsbottom (12)
Earlham High School, Norwich

Limerick

I know a man from Leeds
Who swallowed a packet of seeds
And from his nose
And his toes
Grew half a ton of weeds.

Wayne Parker (13)
Earlham High School, Norwich

My Mum

My mum is loving and caring.
She's so nice, she likes sharing.

Her smile is warm.
She smiles till dawn.

The sun shines bright
When it sees her sight.

The angels sing to Heaven.
Her voice is like bells that ring.

You meet her once
And you want to meet her more.

This loving, caring person
Is guaranteed to be at your door.

She makes you feel wanted.
She makes you feel safe.

Poppy Taylor (14)
Earlham High School, Norwich

The Sea

The deep blue sea,
Mighty and massive,
Waves rushing in,
Fighting and falling!

The vast, watery ocean,
Boats sailing by,
Surfers having the time of their lives,
Swimmers floating by!

Ben Affleck (14)
Earlham High School, Norwich

The Seasons

Flowers bloom,
Birds sing,
Everything so beautiful,
Spring is here.

Sun shining,
Very hot,
At the beach,
Summertime.

Leaves falling,
Animals collect food,
Hibernation,
Autumn time.

White blanket,
Very cold,
Dark afternoons,
Winter's here.

Aaron Curran (14)
Earlham High School, Norwich

The Mighty Reds

Man Utd are the best
And I think can beat the rest.

Van der Sar is a star
And saves the shots from close and far.

Ferdinand is the one
Who stops the attackers one on one.

Ronaldo has the flow
To beat the defenders so well.

The one and only Wayne Rooney
Scores the goal we so need.

Next season we're going to win
The whole thing again.

Kirk Sexton (15)
Earlham High School, Norwich

Who Am I?

I am scatty and skitty
I am always cautious and witty
I am silver and grey
I am furry and if you annoy me
I will surely make you pay.

Who am I?
I love hugs and kisses but only when I dare
Which only includes my family who really, really care
I am liked and loved by all who know me.

Who am I?
I am not adventurous
I am always scared and afraid.

Who am I?
I am Sheba the cat.

Jemma Marjoram (14)
Earlham High School, Norwich

Life Is A Waterslide

Life is like a waterslide
Slow at first then it gets fast.

I often wonder why we were put here
Compared to the giant turtle our life is mere.

Sometimes life is fun, sometimes life is hard
And sometimes life just goes too fast!

But as life closes in you can't help but wonder
When is the reward?

Shaun Talbot (15)
Earlham High School, Norwich

My Worst Subject

English is my worst subject
The teacher's called Miss Hall
All she does is shout and bawl
All I want is her out, out, out
English is my worst subject
The teacher makes me very bored
    If I listen
    If I try
Poor Miss Hall might not cry
    If I listen
    If I try
I won't make poor Miss Hall shout or bawl
    If I listen
    If I try
I can work throughout the day
And never be bored again.

Nathan Moore (14)
Earlham High School, Norwich

Cricket

Cricket is my favourite sport
As it takes a lot of thought
This is because of 3 things
Fielding, bowling and batting

My bowling is quite fast
I try my hardest till the last
My batting is quite good
I wish I was Collingwood

I love my cricket so much
It requires a patient touch
Every Monday I play it
But it does cost a bit.

Steven Guy (14)
Earlham High School, Norwich

Love

When I first saw you
I thought it was just
An angel passing by
Not knowing you were
Meant to be mine.

Each time I look at you
My heart beats, I feel like
I'm falling in love with you.
When you look at me with
Your beautiful eyes, I feel like
I'm falling in a deep, dark
Jungle of love.
I love the colour of your eyes
They are as blue as an ocean
The way you smile, it just
Brings out the colour and the
Beauty of your face.

I like the way you walk
And laugh.
I love your style, girl.

Loveness Muusha (13)
Earlham High School, Norwich

Football!

F ast and speedy
O ver thc post
O ver the crowd
T hrough the gate
B alls, balls everywhere
A hhh! What a goal
L oud went the crowd
L onging for another.

Amber Waller (14)
Earlham High School, Norwich

Jealousy

Every day I sit and weep,
For what I see and cannot keep.
I cannot open this old, worn gate,
To release this anger and the hate.

No matter how much I really care,
This non-returned love I cannot bear.
How much of this I have devoted,
This love I show has now been coated.

In what seems now sheer bitterness,
Spite, envy and watchfulness.
I cannot take this anymore,
Seeing the one I love and adore.

Reaching out for the one I hate,
I finally look away for I cannot wait.
Anymore for the one I love,
I apologise once again, my dove.

I then stumble to my feet,
Reach across to where I meet.
Something that will end this all,
The lights black out and then I fall.

No more pain or hatefulness,
Spite, envy or watchfulness.
As I lie here peacefully,
Seeing now what's happened to me.

Looking back I now regret,
My loves ones I have upset.
There's nothing more for me to see,
For what now has become of me?
Nothing more than jealousy.

Jade Stanton (14)
Earlham High School, Norwich

A Broken Heart

Yesterday we were together
Today we are apart
You came into my life
You touched my heart
I never will forget
The first moment we kissed
And now that you've gone
You will be deeply missed
I thought you loved me
I must have been blind
I thought I had your love
But you left me behind
You gave me warmth
And brightened up my life
But when you left me
It cut me like a knife.

Abie Wilson (15)
Earlham High School, Norwich

One Heart

As I stand near you
My heart goes *boom, boom, boom.*
As I stand near you
My feelings for you mean love not war.
As I stand near you
The wind blows through your hair.
As I stand near you
I whisper in your ear.
As I stand near you
The whisper was nothing much.
As I stand near you
My heart will never stop.
Thump, thump, thump!

Nicole Reynolds (13)
Earlham High School, Norwich

Summer Weather!

Hot, sticky summers warm the air,
Sun staring down, glazing through the air.
Dark clouds gather, blocking the staring sun,
Drops of water falling to the hot floor.
Bolts of lightning striking the floor,
Heavy rain, strong gust of winds scraping through the trees!
Sheet and bolt lightning whizzing through the air,
Dark clouds moving away from the sun.
Distressed electric cloud lighting the sky,
Sun heating the air as well as staring through the air.
The rain stops, heating the air.

Chris Baker (13)
Earlham High School, Norwich

Africa

People are dying in Africa cos they're poor
All we need to do is give them some support
People are dying cos they have no food or clothes
Don't get in a mood cos they have no clue
50,000 people die every day
So make a difference and have your say
A child dies every 3 seconds
So give them something which they beckon
So make a difference and do your bit.

Ashley Lee (14)
Earlham High School, Norwich

I Love You

Roses are red
Violets are blue
If I did not have you
I don't know what I'd do

I love you
And if I die
I will write your
Name on every star
To show everyone how
Much you mean to me.

Stephanie Bullock (15)
Earlham High School, Norwich

The Sandman!

Do you hear creaks at night?
Then do you snuggle up tight?
Do you dare turn on the light?
Sometimes he gives you an awful fright!
Always keep your eyes shut tight!

He's hungry
He wants food
Guess what?
He wants you!

Daniel Smith (12)
Earlham High School, Norwich

Stories Of The Sea

The unpredictable sea,
Sometimes calm, sometimes rough,
The refreshing ripples of crystal clear,
Doesn't happen every day of the year.

The soothing sound of summer breeze,
The rhythmic flow of the ocean,
This is the sound of Heaven,
Brushing the face of a crustacean.

The immeasureable beauty of the surroundings
Is a sight which can't be missed.
But the crashing and thrashing of howling winds
Lets the shoreline rocks be kissed.

Daniel Frazer (12)
Earlham High School, Norwich

A Poem About Ariel

A spirit sent from up above,
Once pure and white amongst a dove,
Set foot upon an evil plan,
Hag-seed hence! A horrid man,
Now's lost the subtle shade of white,
Took off just once, became of night.

Jessica Broad (13)
Great Cornard Middle School, Sudbury

Caliban's Monologue

Prospero is my captor, my owner.
To him I am but a piece of property.
To him I am but a most lying slave.
O' the things I have to endure.
But not for long.
For tonight I will *kill* Prospero,
And in doing so avenge my mother's freedom over this island.
However, his daughter Miranda,
Her name is like a breath of fresh air,
When all hope to breathe again has faded.
Her hair is the colour of daybreak,
And as soft as a sun-kissed cloud,
And every day is *torture* as a lowly beast that I know I am,
But knowing that I will *never* be able to hold her,
Or kiss her head in a comforting way,
Is more unbearable to my *soul* than any torture from Prospero.
That is why, when Prospero is *dead* I can . . .
Wait!
What is that talking above me?
It sounds like men's voices!
Other men?
I'd better go and see . . .

Corrinne Gallop (12)
Great Cornard Middle School, Sudbury

Good Vs Good, Evil Vs Evil

Blistered, hag-born freak,
Lying, deformed, slave creature,
Foot-licking rebel.

Tyrannical warlock,
A cruel disgrace to humanity.
A thieving schemer.

Hag-born!
Human tyrant!
Soul survivor . . .
Loving father . . .

Lonely, poor creature,
How I have taken from you,
Stolen your island.

Daring explorer,
Refusing to bow down,
Never giving up.

I cared for your lonely existence,
I taught you ways to be helpful and kind.

I'm thankful for this but I showed you resistance,
Though I loved you, to good things I was blind.

You refused to learn, all my teaching was wasted.
I tried to help but I was deserted by you.

I was left outside, in the cold and darkness,
To survive the torture you put me through.

Kit Buchanan (13)
Great Cornard Upper School, Sudbury

Prospero

This island is my home
But I am kept imprisoned
I am served to by a monster
By a spirit I am hailed
Creatures crawl by moon and sun
In this strange new world that I have found
Cloud-capped hills and golden sands
The sparkling air and shining sea
Yes, my paradise, the one that is just for me
My sanctuary against the cold outside
Surely this is all I ever wanted?
Surely I could ask for nothing more?
But dear, sweet Miranda knows nothing more
She has never seen any likeness but my own
That deformed deceiver plots against me
Caliban, the monster in my world
The darkness in my heart
As precious time passes by
When lightning splits the sky
The breath of death licks my heels
Fear grips my soul
Which is the way I must go?
Where do I turn for wanted guidance?
Who are these people who invade my home?
Above all others I am myself
This island is my home
My prison cell
What can I do but stand and wait
Until I arrive at Heaven's gate?

Katie Belsey (14)
Great Cornard Upper School, Sudbury

The Island - Cinquains

Island
Midnight mushrooms
Picture of nobody
A thousand twanging instruments
Sweet airs.

Mooncalf
Loves his mother
Monster of the island
Not honoured with a human shape
Plain fish.

Leader
Illusionist
Magical enchanter
Enslaves the people that he meets
Strong-willed.

Hopeful
Easy-going
Loyal to Prospero
Manipulating to others
Servant.

Island
Midnight mushrooms
Picture of nobody
A thousand twanging instruments
Sweet airs.

Rebecca Bulmer (14)
Great Cornard Upper School, Sudbury

The Tempest

The enchanted, mysterious island lies here,
With hissing secrets sounding at ear.
A land of dark paradise where spirits hover,
Sweet Ariel obedient, where Caliban shan't bother.
Prospero, a wise man, a duke with magic ways,
With beautiful daughter Miranda who obeys.
Brother left them to die out of jealousy or spite,
But alas! Revenge is about to strike!
A tempest is planned, for brother Antonio is near on ship,
Waves tower and gobble people up and they flip.
Each passenger is alone on island without a clue,
In a shocked state, not knowing what to do.
Miranda meets prince, they love each other,
But Prospero tests Ferdinand's love for another.
Ariel takes the king and Antonio to Prospero,
Where he would let his evil brother know.
That he forgives him for wanting him dead,
And that his daughter and the prince will soon wed.
Prospero throws his magical books in the sea,
His tricks are no longer needed for he is free.
Ariel is set free because he served well,
While the beast Caliban curses and dwells.
They go back to Milan where they belong,
And live happily together forever long.

Rosie Folan (14)
Great Cornard Upper School, Sudbury

My Life

I look at my island and see;
How lush and lusty the grass looks,
I look at my island and see;
A brave new world,
I look at my island and see;
A thousand twanging instruments,
I look at my island and see;
Midnight mushrooms,
I look at my island and see;
A magical world full of life,
I look at my island and see;
A brave kingdom,
I look at my island and see;
Cloven pine and cloud-cropped towers,
I look at my island and see;
A green new world,
I look at myself and see;
A man of fifty-three.

Emma King (14)
Great Cornard Upper School, Sudbury

The Island

In the distance the island was
Deserted, alone and sad
The boat was collapsing beneath my feet
All was senseless, lost and mad!

We arrived on the island, the boat did not
In this strange climate, wet and hot

Caliban, the ugly beast was he
A monster of no integrity
Ariel I did set her free
A servant she now is to me

Miranda was as good as gold
Her beauty in my eyes will never grow old

In the distance the island was
Deserted, alone and sad
As I made my way back to Milan
I had reason to be glad!

Harriet Livermore (13)
Great Cornard Upper School, Sudbury

Dad

Dad goes off to watch TV and leaves his plate on the table.
I go off to watch TV and leave my plate on the table.
Dad comes back to get a beer and sees my plate on the table.
He jumps up yelling,
'Why did you leave your plate on the table?'
Mum butts in and says, 'But you did.'
Dad, still yelling, shouts, *'I did no such thing!'*
Quickly shoving his plate in the dishwasher.
This usually sets the whole house off.

Simon Manning (12)
Hartismere High School, Eye

Blue

The sky
The clear blue ocean
A field of bluebells

Baby-blue
Cold blue
Warm blue
Soft blue
Ink-blue

Blue is swimming
Without movement
Thinking without real thought
Subconsciously slipping
Into your own
    Dreams
        Thoughts
            And
                Worries.

Rachel Norburn (12)
Hartismere High School, Eye

What Animal?

What animal?
Its head a cloud,
Its neck the Empire State Building,
Its body a rugby ball or even an egg,
Its legs the Eiffel Tower,
Its tail a stalk of celery,
Its tongue a streamer.
What animal?

Giraffe!

Callum Towler (13)
Hartismere High School, Eye

What Am I?

I am as smart as the scientist who made me
And I am installed with a CPT
I am found in computers and phones
And I'm an excuse for a ringtone
I can be cheap and expensive
And I come in all different shapes and sizes
If I break in a maths test it would be a crisis
My fuel is sums
And my pollution, answers
My resolution is go away
Stop hitting me and learn to think
Take time to wink and blink and think
Put pen to paper
Don't become a calculator raper.

Jacob Attenborrow (14)
Hartismere High School, Eye

The Dragon

I'm the wind that blows softly against your face.
I'm the tear that falls from your eye.
I'm the shiver going through your spine.

When you hear my name
You think I am the death from the point of the knight
In shining armour with a sword
Big and fierce.

But think . . . have you ever seen me before?
You probably know of my wings that I spread
And brush the end and the beginning of two worlds at once.

Jo Rodgers (13)
Hartismere High School, Eye

I Opened The Door . . .

I opened the door . . .
The house was spotless
Flawless, soulless
It was like a beautifully
Made corpse
Red roses swooned
In vases
Oranges sat in the fruit bowl a day too
Ripe
The TV always on quietly in the
Background
The smell of freshness swept
Within.

But one day . . .

The fruit in the fridge no longer a day
Too ripe
The TV on mute or switched off
The red roses replaced by cacti and
Plants
The housework slid
The embalmed corpse faded
No longer freshness but dullness
Swept through
It was as though someone was watching, spying, wanting
Them.

Amy Stacey (13)
Hartismere High School, Eye

Haiku

The green, spotted frog
Leaps through crashing waterfalls
Making a big splash.

Grace Hughes (12)
Hartismere High School, Eye

What Tales Does The Sea Hold?

I, the sea, am so very old so with that
A lot of tales I hold
I, the sea, am a roundabout
Windy roads run into me
I, the sea, have hundreds of names
Some call me North Sea, even Mediterranean Sea
I also have a few colours
The Red Sea, Black Sea

Sometimes I'm peaceful
Sometimes I'm restless
In storms I'm a spinning top
Twisting and turning
Drums against the rocks
In the morning I'm a new piece of paper
So calm I forget it all happened

Many ships have had a tragedy on me
They've sunk to the ground
Like a stone in water
I, the sea, am full of creatures
All sorts of fish live in me
They swim in me through
Night and day, going around
Finding their way
Many things are born in me
But many things have died in me.

I, the sea, am very old so with that
A lot of tales I hold.

Emma Ellis (13)
Hartismere High School, Eye

George And The Dragon

It was such a tiring journey,
But now I'm here,
I fought through the storm,
But now I have escaped,
I've found the symbol,
And now I'm on it,
I am here feeling fearless but tired,
I might be too weak to fight.

There is the dragon,
Its fangs fresh with blood,
Let that be its last meal,
As I find its weak spot,
I strike with my lance,
With my last bit of strength,
I close my eyes in hope,
And when I open them,
A blood puddle has formed,
From the wound in its head.

There, above the defeated dragon,
Stands the beautiful princess,
Motionless but confused,
Staring at her wounded beast.

I bow to her but still in shock,
I signal the way to my horse,
She bends down to hug the dragon,
And then stares at me with love.

She tells me that the dragon,
Had kept her from harm,
It had protected her from the symbol's curse,
And she had kept it as a pet.

Jocelyn Berry (13)
Hartismere High School, Eye

Waves

Waves,
Clashing,
Plunging,
Coming in and out like a black adder's tongue.

Waves,
Calm,
Trickling water,
Swaying from side to side like a moving see-saw in the park.

Waves,
Subtle in the day,
Ferocious through the night,
Changing like a chameleon's colourful skin.

Abbie Fulcher (13)
Hartismere High School, Eye

English Homework

My mum usually says,
'Anyone for a shopping spree?'
'Livvy, get down here, it's time for tea.'
'Have you done that homework yet?
The deadline must be met.'

My dad is working from home
And always on the phone
He drinks his coffee all the time
But in the night he has a glass of wine.

My brother's hardly at home
But when he is I have a moan
His music is always too loud
But he always says, 'Loud and proud!'

Livvy Mackay (12)
Hartismere High School, Eye

The Poem About My Family

My mum says, 'Take your school clothes off now.'
She goes to cook our tea for me and my brothers
And feed the fish
Plonk
Plonk
Plonk goes the fish food

Dad says, 'Turn off the lights now!'
While he was on the computer
Mutter
Mutter
Mutter goes on

My brother and sister say, 'Just shut up!'
When they are playing
'Shut up
Shut up
Shut up,' they go.

Nan says, 'Get out with your dirty jeans now!'
While she is washing up
'Take them off.'
Off
Off
Off they go

Grandad says, 'Who wants to come and feed the pigs with me?'
While he gets his jumper on
Oink
Oink
Oink go the pigs.

Joshua Bell-Tye (12)
Hartismere High School, Eye

The Black Sea

Hissing of the sea
A heavy storm flooding ships
In darkness . . . darkness

The waves . . . waterfalls
The minute ship filling up
And sinking . . . sinking

The clouds block the light
Pirates all fall overboard
All but one . . . just one

Weeping in the dark
Tales of the seas take place
Shadow . . . dark shadow

They're going under
Drowning in the dark black sea
Life dying . . . dying.

Ryan Hill (13)
Hartismere High School, Eye

The Possum Poem

What is a possum?
Spine like thistles
Face like a rat
And claws like razors.

Ears like radars
And underneath all those spines
Fur, fur and more fur
Fur as soft as velvet

But worst of all that
It's like trying to find a needle in a haystack.

Ben Luckett (13)
Hartismere High School, Eye

Grandad

He sits on his chair,
Searching through a thousand channels,
Looking for something he likes,
Perhaps a game of football?
Till eventually he finds a game!
But his home team is trailing,
His happiness is fading . . .
He swears and mutters to himself,
And slams his fag in the ashtray,
Till eventually his team score,
And he says, 'What a goal, eh?'
Perhaps this isn't such a bad day!

Alex Frost (12)
Hartismere High School, Eye

What Is An Owl?

Its head a ball of dough,
Its body an upside-down egg,
Its feet like yellow, bony fingers,
Its eyes two black mirrors,
Its neck a vanished shadow,

Until . . .
. . . in flight when it becomes a ghostly, beautiful bird.

Emily Millican (13)
Hartismere High School, Eye

What Is A Dog?

Its head is a rugby ball.
Its body is a fat sausage.
Its legs are Twiglets and
Its tail is a feather duster.

Simone Braybrook (13)
Hartismere High School, Eye

What Is A Parrot?

Its head a little walnut,
Its beak a razor blade,
Its body a tennis ball,
Its feet scaled twigs,
Its eyes beads,
Its tongue like thread
And its colours like the rainbow.

Daniel Rice (12)
Hartismere High School, Eye

A Shark

What is a shark?
Its head is a torpedo, pointy and determined,
Its eyes are buttons, beady and black,
Its body is a submarine, leathery and smooth,
Its teeth are hundreds of knives, shining in the deep.

Sarah Strandoo (13)
Hartismere High School, Eye

As I Walk Along The Shore

Wandering along the shore,
Talking to my friends,
Throwing pebbles into the sea,
And smiling to myself.

Rebecca Pizzey (12)
Hartismere High School, Eye

Identity

My tree is a twisted willow
My flower is a poppy
My river is dry
My mad universe in space
My weapon is a food knife
My shadow is identical to me
My speech rough and twisted
My dream always changing
My scenery the moon's surface.

Jake Field (12)
Hartismere High School, Eye

What Is A Penguin?

Its head, a sliver of bread
Its body, a tuxedo
Its beak, a piece of cake
Its wings, flippers
Its feet, broken eggshells

Nothing is as perfect as the penguin!

Cindy Lai (13)
Hartismere High School, Eye

A Fish

Its body like a rugby ball,
Its mouth like a 'V',
Its scales like a snake's,
Overall it swims everywhere.

Jack Buckmaster (13)
Hartismere High School, Eye

The Day My Life Changed!

That day still lives in my memory,
It scars my memory,
Like a picked scab scars a leg,
The day my world fell apart.

My life was shattered,
Like a glass hitting the floor,
I want to scream,
But why wreck my destroyed world?

I sit staring into space,
I do nothing to stop the time passing by,
While most people are having fun,
I am sat here in the remains of my world.

What have I created?
Why do I bother looking at the mess?
My life is ruined
And I sit here helplessly.

I sit here on the floor,
Crying myself to sleep,
I feel like someone has raked my heart out
And left me here to die.

Laura Bowler (12)
Holy Cross Convent School, Chalfont St Peter

Glow

A glow in the room
Shatters the darkness.
A soft moonlight
Creeping in a window.
A slight light tiptoes
Across the glossy wood floor.
The unfolded glow sleeps till dawn.

Amy Swallow (13)
Holy Cross Convent School, Chalfont St Peter

The Moon

The moon, a glimmering ball of dreams,
It brings light to your nightmares,
Like a candle in the dark,
Without the sun it is the king of light,
Bringing comfort to the darkness.

The stars are its only companion,
Scattered across the sky,
They decorate the bleakness,
Like glowing dots of fire,
Keeping the sky alight.

The moon's shine ripples out,
Casting its rays across the darkness,
Slowly fading as the light rises,
Bringing back the ball of fire,
The new king of the sky.

Lauren Fessey (13)
Holy Cross Convent School, Chalfont St Peter

The Reflective Tree

It quivered, startled, swaying nervously
In the gripping wind like an empty swing
That has been left to dangle in a desolate park.

It trembled ferociously
Like a baby's rattle being hurled across the room.
It shivered feverishly
As it dropped its exquisite garments into the icy cold,
Like a bedridden child throwing off its bed sheets
And being left alone in a damp room to amuse itself
With its own daunting mind.

And as the darkness came down on the wings of the night,
The shrivelled weeping willow whimpered
Under the strain of the moon.

Caitlin Wagstaff (13)
Holy Cross Convent School, Chalfont St Peter

Africa At Its Weakest

'A child dies every three seconds,'
Is what I heard on TV,
Amazing, the destruction of poverty,
Helplessness and anxiety,
Could kill anyone who went to see,
Africa at its weakest!

'Lady Liberty needs glasses,'
Someone once told me,
The world was blind and had a heart of ice,
The promising day has now approached us,
Eight countries uniting to conquer the suffering of,
Africa at its weakest.

'Children are our future,'
But how can that be if they can't live for the present,
Money can be a source of happiness,
But can be selfish and cause misery,
We need to fight the evil debt and help,
Africa at its weakest.

Henna A Sachdev (13)
Holy Cross Convent School, Chalfont St Peter

Stained Glass Perfection

A window is a view of dreams,
A pathway of vision,
To a picturesque scenery outside of you,
But when the window is broken,
The glass is shattered,
Your shattered dreams collapse to the ground,
The scene turns dull and floods with water,
The tears pour out,
And flood the visions of a stained glass perfection,
Open to your dreams,
Are now broken nightmares.

Alex Smith (13)
Holy Cross Convent School, Chalfont St Peter

The Crossroads Of Purgatory

My clothes are saturated with blood
The wine of demons
My mind is full to the brim with light
The truth of angels
I can't remember what it was like to live
And happiness elude
A sacred dream won't fail
Why am I alone?
Isn't this the place
Where the Reaper led me?
The sanctuary of lost souls, forgotten apostles
A hand reaching out for mine
Scared of falling from grace
Why am I so afraid?
But why bite the hand that's trying to save me?
Is this Heaven or is this Hell?
Am I on the plane of tangled hearts
Intertwining memories, decaying dreams?
I'm running from everlasting light
To forever bleak, unending night
Falling into darkness
Drowning my fears
Smothered by my sorrows
What were hopes for tomorrow
Are now continuous tears
Loneliness is so consuming
As I curl up here to die
Paradise is so confusing
Maybe I'll just say goodbye.

Helen Mulhall (13)
Holy Cross Convent School, Chalfont St Peter

I Feel

I felt sad, I felt alone,
Stone-cold, so wrong,
I felt unhappy, didn't believe,
I wanted to be free, let out
Of my cage, my prison.

Then it happened, the thing
I prayed for came true,
My hopes were coming true,
All I had wanted, came true.

But it was too good to be true,
Back to my prison, my dark cage,
But, a glimmer of hope in my dark passing,
Still hoping.
My dream came true, my fantasy,
I feel complete.

Frances Bate (12)
Holy Cross Convent School, Chalfont St Peter

What Is Blue?

Blue is the sky
Up very high
Blue is feeling down in the dumps
Crying my eyes out
Sometimes blue
Is a blue bluebell!

Blue is like bands
Singing the blues
Blue is relaxing
Like the deep blue sea
Blue is like a dolphin
Who swims in the sea!

Blue is what I wear
Which suits me best!

Hannah Curtis (12)
John Colet School, Wendover

Homecoming

Sick and tired of my existence
So much it doesn't hurt anymore
I look out the window
To see him walk past
Makes my heart break
Now I want to cry
I can't feel pain
Apart from the emotions
Which get stretched
And are bigger, stronger
You can't make me this way
Not anymore
Not at all
I just want to get home
With friends and family
So I can once more be happy
To feel giggly, to cry with laughter
I want to go home
I'm surrounded by a hundred different tears
Pouring down
I'm done as I wipe away the last tear
As I open the door
I'm here
I'm home.

Danielle Smith (14)
Oriel High School, Great Yarmouth

The Battle Of Middle Earth

The arrows flew straight past me and hit the men behind me.
And I heard the painful scream of poison.
The Orks are mouldy pigs at war.
The explosives on their backs were big fireworks.
The fearless cannibals are creatures with armour.
The shields are cymbals clashing with rage.
The castle is a small war ground with millions of warriors.

Kyle Glennon (11)
Riverside Middle School, Bury St Edmunds

Pocket Stuff

'Shane! Look at the state your trousers are in
Covered in mud, oh I really can't win.
Empty your pockets, take out all your stuff.
Oh! Keys, a pen, money and gum. Did you take enough?
Shane, why have you a screwdriver at all?
Did you plan to take the school blackboard off the wall?'

'Oh, Mum, don't go on, I need rubber bands.
Am I expected to hold all in my hands?
And shoelaces in shoes are just not cool,
So I keep them in pockets, I'm no fool.
Mum, I do understand that KitKats melt,
But I couldn't keep it under my belt.

Why doesn't everybody understand I'm not manky?
I need lots of things, even a bogie-filled hanky.
Why do they make pens that leak?
Even if I leave them in my pocket for a week.
Pockets are not only for money, you know,
They are for sweet papers and balls to throw.'

'Mother, leave Shane alone, I understand,
When I was a young man I carried more than a band.
Paper clips and matches, a penknife too,
But today those things you just don't do.
Boys do carry a lot of stuff,
And pockets are handy, just not big enough.'

Shane Carter (11)
Riverside Middle School, Bury St Edmunds

Aliens

The kids in my school are all aliens and came here from Mars.
They all have antennas that stick out of their brains.
They walk around the school being rude and holding grudges.
They got on their ship and came here from Mars.
Although, when there's a new kid, they're one of a kind.

Amber McLaren (11)
Riverside Middle School, Bury St Edmunds

My Rabbit

My rabbit is a lump of snow falling from the sky
My rabbit is an elf grinning from ear to ear
My rabbit is a funny munchkin that makes a smelly mess
My rabbit is a grumpy camel waiting for its food
My rabbit is a long-eared giraffe
That has just flown down from Mars
My rabbit is a woodpecker when it is waiting for its drink
My rabbit is a fluff of fun.

Jodie Newton (11)
Riverside Middle School, Bury St Edmunds

The Fireball

The sun is a big ball filled with light bulbs.
The sun is a red snooker ball.
The sun is an over-bright lantern.
The sun is a flame on the stove.
The sun is a red-faced, rampaging man.
The sun is a planet of madness.
The sun is a murderer.
The sun is a call from Hell.

Christopher Willis (11)
Riverside Middle School, Bury St Edmunds

Wrestling

The Rock is strong and stylish
Stacy Keibler's car is fast and wicked
A headlock is Hell in a cell
Stone Cold is undefeatable
Rob Van Dam has cool, fast moves
Rey Mysterio is a lightweight
The Kane is a monster.

Jason Sperrink (11)
Riverside Middle School, Bury St Edmunds

Untitled

(Inspired by a quote from John Ruskin, 'If some people really see angels where others see empty space, let them paint the angels . . .')

If some see angels where others see space
Where the governed mind cannot see the light
Let us paint the angels in all the grace

Tedious reality has encased
Imagination's escape in its flight
If some see angels where others see space

Though we may find paths we wish to retrace
So we are not alone through the night
Let us paint the angels in all their grace

Those who have come to pass that Holy place
Have felt the presence and their bright light
If some see angels where others see space

When despair and heartache have interlaced
When we heard their mournful cry and plight
Let us paint the angels in all their grace

Where is the poetry of life's embrace?
It has all been but spent save one last sight
If some see angels where others see space
Let us paint the angels in all their grace.

Natacha Killin (17)
St Bernard's High School, Westcliff-on-Sea

Flying Alone

Flying alone through this turbulent storm
With one wing half severed, and the other torn
Encased in darkness, a slave of the night
The stars dictate my path of flight.
Gliding across these changing borders
Unleashed to explore the foreign land
I roam this Earth, without a plan
In my heart the headstone is finally at rest
For the aborted child, that once was blessed
In my wake I enter new domain
I must mend my wings and rise again.

Soon the journey will end and the shadows descend
And the sun make an entrance, whilst a new quest is penned
A fresh lease of life from a band of light will ascend
I'll leave my demons to rest, a new day I'll spend
With my angels. Flying alone no more.

Rebecca D'Souza (17)
St Bernard's High School, Westcliff-on-Sea

Death, Destruction, Poverty

These words we hear send shivers down my spine,
I know we try hard,
But why is Africa still living in the pain
Of poverty?
We hear words from Bob Geldof,
'We must help Africa'.
We do, nothing changes,
Think of the people at the G8 summit,
What must be going through their minds?
But I say this to them,
Remember this, leaders of the world, *click*,
That's a child dying, *click*,
A child dies every three seconds in Africa,
From *poverty*.

Alice McParlane (13)
St Clement Danes School, Chorleywood

The World

The world is precious
The world is polluted

If you speak in a crowd and no one hears you,
Did you speak?

If the world suffers and weeps and you ignore it,
Is it suffering and weeping?

The world is being poisoned
Like a drop of ink spilt onto a piece of paper.
The world is being polluted like a wave crashing onto the shore
Like a titan in its wake,
Swallowing the sand and shells beneath it.
The titan is being unleashed and we must fight to stop it,
We must join forces and form a wall of defence
Like a wall of white blood cells
Fighting off the bacteria attacking our bodies.

The world is speaking and it is being ignored.

The world is precious
The world is polluted.

Elliott Day (13)
St Clement Danes School, Chorleywood

Life!

Life!
Family, friends and relatives, I like, I do, I do.
God, neighbours and television, I like, I do, I do.
People I've never met, strangers and you,
I'm not sure about, I'm not, I'm not.
Danger, happiness and excitement, are daily felt.
My opinions are strong, they are, they are.
I know many people, I do, I do.
Nelson Mandela is my hero.
My first love is sport, I say, I say.
Except it's too hot to play, today.

Oscar O'Mara (13)
St Clement Danes School, Chorleywood

The Human Mind

My mind is like a ticking clock,
Slowly clicking out of time,
Knowing no safe haven,
But constantly under assault,
From emotion terrorists and secrets,
That could explode in their own time.

They could be a fly,
Insignificant but pestering,
Or maybe an elephant,
Bold and inspiring.

However,
What we do not know is this,
Day in and day out,
We are subject to this merciless cycle,
As it kills us slowly,
Emotionally and physically,
And as we seek to escape our own fate,
Our minds eventually overcome us all.

Fenton Tinkler (13)
St Clement Danes School, Chorleywood

My Love

I saw a beautiful girl standing in my garden.
I said, 'You don't belong in here.'
She said, 'I beg your pardon?'
I said, 'This place is my garden,
What are you doing here?'
She said, 'Ah, then I must be lost,'
And then, 'Oh dear, oh dear, oh dear.'

Matt Hinge (13)
St Clement Danes School, Chorleywood

Hunting A Hare

As the sun goes down,
He starts to move quicker and quicker,
Turning his head towards the sounds.

Running swiftly in the night,
Chasing towards his prey in excitement,
Slowing down as it comes into sight.

Camouflaged in the fresh green grass,
Licking his lips hungrily,
Knowing the prey is within his grasp.

Advancing towards the hare,
Getting lower and lower,
His teeth are bared.

Ready to pounce,
Here we go,
With one big bounce.

And one big roar,
Not knowing what's happening,
It was under his claws.

Colin Spooner (12)
St Clement Danes School, Chorleywood

The Living Of The Forest

The living of the forest
The whisper in the trees
The whistle of the wind
Gets caught up in their leaves.

The living of the forest
The burrows go deep down
But at the very black of night
Footprints stain the ground.

The living of the forest
The river rushing by
Glides like a restless ghost
And emits an eerie cry.

The forest is still living
Trees will still grow high
Because this silent setting
The forest will never die.

Ross Kershaw (13)
St Clement Danes School, Chorleywood

Family And Friends

Friends are here to stay
Even when they go away
A secret told is a secret kept
When your secret was out
Your heart never wept
But when worst comes to worst
Your friends always come first

Your mother's love is unconditional
Even when your faults are unforgivable
Your family is there to help you up
When you are down and feel like giving up
From time to time you need their love
Sent from Heaven by a dove
Think closely about your mother's unconditional love.

Lizzy Eames (13)
St Clement Danes School, Chorleywood

Missing The Things About Grandad

Smart and pristine in a tie and
Braces covered his hippo belly,
A little tickle made him giggle,
His face crinkled, still soft and round.
Grandma sat all stressed and worried
Until that giggle made everyone glad.

Bouncy and bubbly,
Cute and cuddly,
His friendly way and warm heart,
Made him a special part.

Relaxed he smiled,
In the snug, tinged green chair,
Calm he sat, as calm as an angel.
Snoring, mimicking the sound of Heaven.

Bouncy and bubbly,
Cute and cuddly,
His friendly way and warm heart,
Made him a special part.

Lucy Rose McIntosh (13)
St Clement Danes School, Chorleywood

Friendship

Friendship is like a rose,
It gives birth, blooms and eventually dies.
Friends are the angels in your life, except they don't have wings.
What would we do if we didn't have friends?
Would we laugh?
Would we cry?
Would we love and respect people who weren't our relations?
Friendship, as fragile as a feather,
Floating in the wind,
Flittering in the air.
Friendship is like a rose,
It gives birth and dies.

Nina Boniface (13)
St Clement Danes School, Chorleywood

Battle

Screaming and shouting
My enemy comes.
Too many to count, too many to see,
They were the grains of sand on the beach.

The glitter of evil rested upon their blades,
Death, destruction lay behind them.
Peace and prosperity lay ahead,
While I was in the middle, alone.

I felt the anger surge through me,
Like a river breaking through a dam.
I gripped the shining blade,
Then roared to the heavens.

I ran, I ran at them with my eyes only seeing them.
Nothing would stop me, nothing.
The first one came in all his disgusting glory.
My blade went through him, he would kill no more.

Death and blood, death and blood,
The shouts and cries of battle and death.
I broke upon them like the sea upon the beach,
Gradually eroding the shore.

I could not see through the enemy to the joy within,
For I would die, like the world I knew before this,
I would revenge those before me,
I would take them down with me, they would kill no more.

Alun Jones (13)
St Clement Danes School, Chorleywood

The Day That Was A Broken Misery

The way you acted,
Destroyed her, destroyed her life,
For a while she thought the world would break,
Fall apart.
Your apology was a hidden secret that was never heard.
Your voice, full of the facts, ran through her body like,
Blood from a wound.
You didn't care for her, you did wrong,
But yet it was still her soul pleading sorrows of forgiveness,
For your mistakes! She knew what you did was blind,
Happiness, but pain is a ghost to everyone except she.
Her pain could never be heard, her pain was a locked door,
Never to be opened.
Sometimes, she was punished, punished for honesty.
And still she pleads, pleads for her old life back, a life
Without trace or memory of events that froze her mind
And broke her world!

Charlotte O'Reilly (13)
St Clement Danes School, Chorleywood

The Perfect Storm

As we walked across the mellow fields,
Darkness filled the sky.
Many tiny raindrops,
Fell upon our heads.

As the wind began to howl,
Like a dog wanting food.
The lightning made an energy,
More powerful than the sun.

Then out of nowhere,
Bang, bang, bang!
You could not hear a thing.
Then a sudden ring,
But nothing around to make it.

Tom Hewitt (13)
St Clement Danes School, Chorleywood

Nelson Mandela

Nelson Mandela, he fought and he fought,
Determination or courage, he was never short.
Twenty-seven years of his life he spent in a cell,
Isolated, alone - those years were hell.
Silent, secluded: sinister and small,
The walls were cold, grey and tall.
The shout of the guards was routine day and night,
Sometimes he would see blood, gore or an inhumane sight.
Each morning he worked with a hammer and stone,
While guards bellowed at him in a very aggressive tone.
As the years went by, life became rougher,
But Mandela hung on and grew even tougher.
And now he is free, his years in prison finished,
He fought and he fought and his suffering is diminished.

David Grant (13)
St Clement Danes School, Chorleywood

The Unknown Being

(Inspired by 'Granny' by Spike Milligan)

Its outstretched hands and beady eyes,
In the night, its piercing cries,
Its elegant yet mysterious prowl,

This creature is not known to man . . .

Hunting for its prey all through the night
Waiting for the time that's right.
Strike, scratch, thud, bang! It's dead.

This creature is not known to man . . .

A silhouette is all you see,
Between the leaves, between the trees.
A dark shadow covers the land.

This creature is not known to man . . .

Charlotte Bodley (13)
St Clement Danes School, Chorleywood

Child War

I said to my mother one gloomy night
That no matter what happened I was prepared to fight
Be it for my family, country or even my right.

She stood still like an old, oak tree
Not saying a thing until I counted to three
She stuttered and said, 'What are you trying to be?

So gallant and brave
You stupid child, you'll go straight to your grave
And please be aware that you won't be saved.'

I glared into space
As I packed my suitcase
All I could think of was that I was saving my race.

I gradually opened the door
My mother, as if blind, just looked at the floor
She looked up and like a fountain began to pour.

'Go if you must
But hatred, fear and fighting can never be just
Better love, hope, peace and trust.'

Alice Denyer (13)
St Clement Danes School, Chorleywood

The Storm

A storm is brewing.
Thick, black clouds and loud, clapping thunder,
Blinding lightning too.
Pit, pat, pit, pat,
Tiny raindrops bigger and bigger,
Heavier and heavier.
Thou art shivering as lightning strikes.
It is all quiet, nothing, apart from rain whipping the windows.
Then, out of nowhere, a huge fork of lightning,
Strikes the ground,
Followed instantly by a huge clap of thunder.
Everything is silent, rain becoming gentler, gentler.
Thunder getting further and further away,
Dragging rain and lightning with it.
Everything is now silent.
Silent.
Silent.

Holly Fitch (13)
St Clement Danes School, Chorleywood

My Journey Around The World

I went all the way to China just
To see a wall
I went all the way to New York
Just to visit the mall
I went all the way to south London
To see a leopard gecko
I went all the way to north Blackpool
To see all the art deco
I travelled back to the 60s
Just to see a hippy
And then I took my kid to school
And saw him being lippy!
So to round it up (if you can bear to listen)
In this competition I hope my poem will glisten!

Douglas McAteer (13)
St Clement Danes School, Chorleywood

Why?

There are good
And there are bad
In this world - who do we turn to?
Life's a story
A fantasy dream
The world's a myth
A puppet on strings
Everyone tangled
Black and white
A mesh-grey
Why?
Why were we put on this world of war?
Why?
There is life
And there is death
We want answers - who do we turn to?
Life's a question
A winding stream
Death's a myth
A labyrinth of dreams
Everyone tangled
Black and white
A mesh-grey
Why?
Why are we dying to live but living to die?
Why?

Alexandra Shapland (13)
St Clement Danes School, Chorleywood

The Beach

The golden star of sand,
In the shape of a mighty hand.
The giant dog-like waves,
Force themselves against the caves.

The gentle breeze,
On a mountain of trees.
The claws of a crab,
Getting ready to grab.

The murky, black seaweed,
Buried beneath the salty seabed's surface of weeds.
For the sunbathers there is silence,
All around them is no violence.

The beaming sun,
Gleaming on the joyful fun.
The swiftly moving silverfish,
With them you can make one wish.

Sandcastles built up high,
Whispering to the sky:
'Oh mighty cloud,
Won't you come down,
To see the glistening beach?'

Carrie Udall (13)
St Clement Danes School, Chorleywood

When I Was A Little Girl

When I was a little girl,
Only the age of three,
My daddy was a fireman,
He used to cuddle me.
He was as tall as a skyscraper,
As soft as a teddy bear,
He risked his life for people,
But Daddy didn't care.

When I was a little girl,
Now the age of seven,
My mummy was a teacher,
She used to work in Devon.
She was as clever as a scientist,
As delicate as a china doll,
She taught children their ABCs,
And cared within her soul.

And now I am all grown up,
The age of twenty-three,
I'm working as a teacher,
First my mum, then me.
I'm as smart as my mum,
Like Dad, I'm brave,
And when I go to Heaven,
I'd like 'Daddy's girl' on my grave.

Samantha Blake (13)
St Clement Danes School, Chorleywood

Abusing Animals

Animals big and small,
Animals short and tall,
Animals as tall as a tower,
Animals as small as a flower,
Animals are everywhere,
But no one gives a care,
Animals dying,
Animals crying,
Animals kicked,
Animals sick,
Animals dead,
Animals not fed,
Animals poached,
Animals lives encroached,
Animals kept in cages,
Animals left alone for ages,
Animals with fear in their eyes,
Animals that let out long cries,
Animals are living things too,
Just like me and you.

Gemma Holloway (13)
St Clement Danes School, Chorleywood

Who Was It?

Silently she walks,
Slowly she talks,
Secretly wondering,
Who is it?

A bang on the door,
She falls on the floor,
Silently screaming,
Who is it?

She lays with a blank face,
With a heart that used to race,
With a smile that faded,
She lays.

Her eyes roll around,
While lying on the ground,
Not moving an inch,
Who was it?

Ed Houghton (13)
St Clement Danes School, Chorleywood

Games

Here's some info about games.
We already know they're really cool.
Most of them have lots of aims.
To not play them you would be a fool.
There's Crash Twinsanity,
And Extreme G,
Jake 3,
And Dragonball Z.
Some are novice, some advanced.
There are lots of different modes
So take a chance.
Some have save and load
So get some food and get your mates,
And play the game to test your fate.

Sean Walden (12)
St John Fisher RC School, Peterborough

My Beautiful Car!

The love that I have for my beautiful car
How fast it goes I do not know
All I know is that it goes quite far
I wait for the flag man to say, 'Go, go, go!'

The red paint on the car sparkles in the dazzling sun
Then the clouds come by and it starts to rain
The roof closes faster than the shot of a gun
Then the rain cools the car and more energy it gains.

I skidded fast around the bend
I got out the car and went in the shop
I asked a man if ten pence he could lend
For all I wanted to buy was a lollipop.

So back in the car I went
And forgot to give back the ten pence he lent.

Antonio De Miranda (12)
St John Fisher RC School, Peterborough

The Dark Is . . .

An old man's funeral
Haunted by a zombie's cry,
A screaming child
Awaiting the darkness beneath the stairs,
Lucifer's laugh
From a raging flame,
A murder in the dead of night
Followed by a horrific sight.

Joseph Coombe-Boxall (13)
St John Fisher RC School, Peterborough

The Dark Is . . .

The Devil's heart
The soul of a murderer
The eye of a thief
The mind of Satan

The fur on a panther
A bottomless pit
A never-ending tower
The laugh of a killer

The dead of night
A haunted house
The scream of the dead
The dark is *evil.*

David Tyrrell (13)
St John Fisher RC School, Peterborough

The Dark Is . . .

A walk in the forbidden woods
With wolves lurching for their prey.

Cemetery at midnight
With an unknown tomb.

A full moon, hiding in the dark clouds.
Simply Satan's Heaven.

A vampire's thirst for blood.
The disturbing sights you see at night.

The dark is . . .
. . . the world.

Ceri Mattless (13)
St John Fisher RC School, Peterborough

My Modified Sonnet

Shall I compare you to a modified car?
But you are more stylish and expensive:
Rain and winds may go far,
But hail and ice will not be corrosive.
Many paints and different accessories
Add to your fair, heavenly complexion.
Though the garage brings out the money fees,
You turn heads on the motorway section.
Even though your paint may fade
A respray will help and fix.
It'll save you from the dodgy trade
And it will only take two ticks.
    So as long as people cry or people brag,
    As long as all of this, your beauty will not sag.

James Chapman (13)
St John Fisher RC School, Peterborough

Alliteration

One wild wolf wailed wandering in the woods.
Two tumblewood tigers tumbled towards the town.
Three thick thugs thumped through therapy.
Four fairies fainted from the fear of feeling flesh.
Five famished flies fidgeted frantically.
Six silly snakes got stuck in sauce.
Seven sucking centipedes sucked someone's soul.
Eight anxious elephants angrily argued.
Nine nasty nannies naughtily knitted neat neck braces.
Ten tedious tortoises tickled tediously.

Nick Webb (13)
St John Fisher RC School, Peterborough

Poem

Friends are forever
Friendship made to last
Friends stay together
For the future as well as the past

I'm a friend forever
I'm here to stay
If we work together
We can keep it that way

Tell me all your secrets
I will share mine too
If you ever need any help
I'm here to help you

If you have read this read it again
And remember *you are my friend.*

Marlerne Smith Star (13)
St John Fisher RC School, Peterborough

Problems . . .

The sky is blue
The clouds are white
I have a flu
But I feel alright
It's nice and sunny
And way too hot
But my nose is runny
And my stomach is a knot
I went to bed
At half-past eight
But the doctor said,
'Don't sleep too late.
Get up at five
If you want to stay alive.'

Fezan Akhtar (13)
St John Fisher RC School, Peterborough

The Dark Is . . .

The dark is like a nightmare,
Full of spooks and scares.
Ghosts and ghouls around every corner,
And lots more surprises on the way!

The dark is in the graveyards,
With the dead people buried in the ground.
In the day it's peaceful and calm,
But at night, all the dead come out to play!

The dark is like Hell,
And all the sun surrounding it.
The only light inside,
Is the flames burning people alive!

So be careful,
Because the dark is everywhere!

Hannah Bolton (13)
St John Fisher RC School, Peterborough

Nature

One weird whale had a whale of a time,
Two tangled tigers tumbled into a typhoon,
Three thick thieves thumped into a theatre,
Four fishes fought ferociously,
Five famished fleas fidgeted,
Six swans sat in the sea,
Seven slushy strawberries sent shocking signals,
Eight eccentric elephants ate eagerly,
Nine naughty newts nested near Northumbria,
Ten tedious tortoises tackled tigers.

Leigh-Anne Dodds (13)
St John Fisher RC School, Peterborough

Shall I Compare You To the Moon . . .

Shall I compare you to the moon
That only shines at night?
It's all day that I hope to see you soon
It's all day that you're out of my sight
Your beauty I see in my dreams
You make the whole night sky shine
The night's not long enough, that's how it seems
You look so fine
You make the stars twinkle
You take away the darkness
Your beauty you sprinkle
It is your beauty we all suss
I love you, my dear
And I do not fear!

Fazeela Akram (13)
St John Fisher RC School, Peterborough

F1

In his F1 car he will go far
Driving so fast he won't be last
The fans are going wild
The others are just riled
Because there is only one more mile
And has been in the lead for quite a while
As he goes past the finish line
Out comes the wine
1st is Schumacher, 2nd Barricello and 3rd Alonso
What a great day, he earned his pay
A smile on his face as he ends the race
And proved no one could keep up with his pace.

Tony Baldo (12)
St John Fisher RC School, Peterborough

Resident Evil

Can I fix this world of war?
The smell of death hanging through the air,
All the bodies, blood, guts and gore,
More of them are coming, we must prepare!

We've received news about the big one,
It will be here by dawn,
They are going to drop a nuclear bomb,
In this game of chess, I feel like a pawn,

There is nothing I can do to stop it,
The world as we know it will end,
But even pawns can make the bright side lit,
My team needs help, a hand I will lend.

We've no choice but to run,
I'm not staying for goodness sake,
The break of dawn has come,
And no one can stop my last escape . . .

Thomas Harwin (13)
St John Fisher RC School, Peterborough

Fire And Death

Fire is like a slow death
It takes forever
It takes its time
It makes water fall from people's eyes
The worst colour to wear is black
All you are left with is ashes.

Natasha Butler (12)
St John Fisher RC School, Peterborough

Pool

I wanna play pool,
But my mama isn't cool,
I wanna go pro,
But my mama says no!

My mates are down the hall,
Potting all the balls,
I'm stuck in my room,
In the house of doom!

They rang and said, 'Joe,
Where did you go?'
I've got a new cue,
I don't know what to do!

I wanted to play pool,
And now I look a fool!

Joseph Hostead (13)
St John Fisher RC School, Peterborough

The Sun Is . . .

A fiery ball of heat
Light throughout the galaxy
A red, fiery cricket ball
An expanding world of knowledge
A gaseous, smelly annoyance
An undefeatable sphere
A fireman's nightmare
A massive lava volcano
A gas giant
The centre of the galaxy.

Michael Wiles (12)
St John Fisher RC School, Peterborough

Rita Queen Of Speed

Nervously awaiting,
Clutching the bar,
Heartbeat a-pounding,
Sat in the car.

When all of a sudden,
Darkness prevails,
We're shooting forward,
Clattering on rails.

Oh what have I done?
My mind starts to shout,
I can't stay on,
I've got to get out.

But then as we reach,
The final corner,
I let out a shout,
Thank God it's over.

Daniel O'Connell (12)
St John Fisher RC School, Peterborough

The World

How can I walk tall
When the streets are crying and
Children are dying?
What's going on with the world today?
Tears on my pillow every night.
We've got to find peace
Before everybody turns obese.
Keep your head up.
Keep the faith up.

Flora Chiutsi (12)
St John Fisher RC School, Peterborough

A Rotten Leaf

Should I compare you to a rotten leaf,
That falls on the ground in the autumn?
Because that's what you are, a rotten leaf,
And you will eventually get your portion.

The leaf will just rot in the sun,
As you rot the life of another.
Everyone is trying to have fun,
Then you come with the darkening cover.

People will get madder and madder,
And you will try and run.
But all those people's lives you made sadder and sadder,
Will come and take your fun.

Within these people you will have met your match
And you will never make a sound,
Because you'll be in an unused patch
Where you will never be found.

Matthew Weston (13)
St John Fisher RC School, Peterborough

A Dog

A dog is like a rainy day,
But only when it feels down,
A dog is like a sunny day,
But only when it plays the clown,
A dog is like a snowy day,
But only when it's in a mood,
A dog is like a windy day,
But only when it barks for food,
A dog is expensive, you have to pay,
A dog is for life not just Christmas Day.

Georgia Farrimond (13)
St John Fisher RC School, Peterborough

Broken Heart

The hours go past,
Whilst I think of you.
Time goes so fast,
I don't know what to do.

I'm stuck to think,
Of what I can stop.
We first met at the ice rink,
We still do talk a lot.

I still remember our first date,
My heart pounded.
It was fate,
Then I was grounded.

Now you have left,
I'm free!

Mariana Mancellos (13)
St John Fisher RC School, Peterborough

My Life - Haiku

Death walks and I die
Walk in Heaven, my life ends
I'm alive at last.

Steven Fairbrace (12)
St John Fisher RC School, Peterborough

The Sea - Haiku

Waves crashing on rocks
White sea horses riding waves
This king is the sea.

Katie King (12)
St John Fisher RC School, Peterborough

Sandra Smith

Sandra Smith,
Was pure and kind.
Some say this is a myth,
But it's all in their minds.

She was walking through an alleyway,
Late in the night,
After a long and exhausting day,
She saw a traumatic sight.

It was a large and rough figure,
That made her pulse race,
The shadow grew bigger and bigger,
She then ran, getting ready for a chase.

After getting stabbed she bled and bled
Until she could bleed no more,
And then she was found the next morning,
Dead on the floor.

Johnson Platinum (13)
St John Fisher RC School, Peterborough

Pork!

A lady while dining in York,
Once found out she really liked pork,
She wanted some more,
And had a whole boar,
But it wouldn't all fit on her fork!

Jessica Guy (12)
St John Fisher RC School, Peterborough

Beware, Yeah?

He'll meet you and sweep you off your feet,
He's nice, he's funny, so cute and so sweet,
He's the perfect guy, the one of your dreams,
You belong together . . . or so it seems.

You ditch your friends for your new obsession,
You don't realise your future is full of depression,
You think you love him, you give him your heart,
Little do you know, he'll tear it apart.

You're right where he wants you, he moulds you like clay,
You see him with girl number three next day,
He's got what he wanted, accomplished his goal,
But he still has your heart that he easily stole.

All you wanted was to have some fun,
Now you wish that it hadn't begun,
You wish one day, you'll see him cry,
Then he'll know how he killed you inside.

He looks in your eyes and plays with your hair,
He tells you that he will always be there,
His touch is so soft, his hold is so tight,
His words are soothing, his kiss is just right.

Beware of players, they'll steal your heart,
And they'll give it back, all torn apart,
Don't let them suck you into their game,
Because once you lose, you're never the same.

Chloë Foster (13)
St John Fisher RC School, Peterborough

Fire

A burning ball of fire,
Makes noises like a choir,
It's really hot like a boiling pot,
The choking, smelly smoke,
Runs down, deeper through your throat.

Ella Foreman (12)
St John Fisher RC School, Peterborough

Why I Love My Boyfriend

My boyfriend's eyes are nothing like a disco ball,
His mouth is as small as an ant,
His teeth have all fallen out, he must have had a fall,
He smells as bad as smelly pants.

His cheeks blow up when he talks,
And his face looks like a baboon,
He stumbles every time he walks,
And when someone tells a joke, he always laughs too soon.

His hair looks like a mop,
And his nails look like they're about to rot,
His clothes are out of fashion, he needs to find new shops,
And every time I look at his nose, I can always see some snot.

But he makes me smile, he makes me laugh,
He's got a great personality,
He's always happy,
I love him and he loves me.

Charlotte Whitwood (11)
St John Fisher RC School, Peterborough

Racism

From dusk till dawn,
You will see all races.
From eve till nightfall,
You will see all faces.
Black or white,
Weight or height,
Don't let racism fright.
>   *Stand up!*
>   *Speak up!*

Esther Beard (12)
St John Fisher RC School, Peterborough

Shall I Compare You?

Shall I compare him to a doll?
His mouth is always still, no words -
His nose is as long as a pole,
His spiky hair always scares the birds.

His skin is as rough as a turtle's shell,
His fingers are like claws,
His perfume is a nasty smell,
He smells like dogs' wet paws.

He sounds like a foghorn,
He sings very bad,
He walks like something that's never been born,
Yes, he's extremely sad!

But however bad he is,
Make sure he never reads this!

Ciaran Hyland (12)
St John Fisher RC School, Peterborough

How Memories Fade . . .

I look back on the years you made me cry.
I thought about the ten times you said goodbye.
Hearing your voice play back in my mind,
The shouting, the anger were not all kind.
You used to play me like a game of Monopoly.
I never was ever your property.
Can you remember the upsetting times you made?
I can, even though I try to make them fade.

Sacha Said (13)
St John Fisher RC School, Peterborough

The Dark Is . . .

The pathway to evil
The crude prank
Opposite to light
An alternative world . . .

Satan's fashion
A little girl's nightmare
Hidden, waiting to strike
An alternative world . . .

Everyone's weakness
The sleeping power
A life changer
An alternative world . . .

For everybody to fear
Life's twisted sister
The shady character
An alternative world . . .

Everyone fears the darkness
Even the tough guy at the bar
Everyone has a little fearfulness
That's why we never get far.

Christopher White (13)
St John Fisher RC School, Peterborough

The Dark Is . . .

Like an old man's funeral,
Interrupted by a zombie's cry.

A rotting corpse with
The Devil's heart.

A screaming child awaiting
The darkness under the stairs.

A murder in the dead of night,
Followed by a horrific sight.

Nick M Webb (13)
St John Fisher RC School, Peterborough

The Boxing King

You're ready, you're ready
You're a champion, you're a legend.
You're Roy Jones Junior!
You walk up to the ring, dressed in blue.
Your opponent gets in the ring, with no clue.
Off goes the bell, *ding, ding, ding,*
Knowing that he is the boxing king.
Now you're having a big spar, one hit, two hit,
You get him to the ground, in no bit.
The referee is counting . . . 5, 6, 7, 8, 9, 10.
The crowd is cheering, when he shouts ten.
You're a winner, you're a champion.

You take your gloves off so proud
And finally both boxers give each other a big bow.

Sam Stanford (13)
St John Fisher RC School, Peterborough

A Poem About Sports!

I don't much like school - I like sports -
I play football and games of all sorts -
There's golf and there's cricket,
I must take this wicket,
Before I get muddled by thoughts . . .
Of my next stunning result,
At basketball or pole vault,
Oh, I must settle to one sport
Or another!

Stefan Salerno (12)
St John Fisher RC School, Peterborough

Hospital Troubles

I once met a man in plaster,
He'd never run from the hospital faster,
He'd heard a chainsaw,
And footsteps on the floor,
So he split like a dog for its master.

He told me his leg it was sprained,
Though a lot of rest he obtained,
From work a short break,
At home, missing steak,
So both good and bad things were gained.

Hannah Johnson (12)
St John Fisher RC School, Peterborough

Schooldays

What will be happening today?
What lessons will I be dreading?
I have got my SATs in May
Many teachers will be meddling
What marks will I be getting
On the work that I'm not doing
And the homework that I'm completing?
With the teachers I'll be meeting
That will also change my seating
Because they think I am cheating
With fellow students I will be competing.

Chantelle Woodbine-Bogle (12)
St John Fisher RC School, Peterborough

Destruction!

They swarm like bees,
They cut down trees,
To raise their taxes,
They come with axes,
They cut them down,
Right down to the ground,
They hear them scream,
They don't care,
Not for insect or bear,
All they want is money,
All the bees love their honey,
Destruction, destruction, destruction!
It's their only satisfaction.

Abdullah Bhatti (13)
St John Fisher RC School, Peterborough

Night

A star's bed
A vampire's safety
The day's rival
A dark, black blanket
A sea of destruction
Never-ending space
Long, overflowing, black water
Someone's phobia.

Ballal Seddique (13)
St John Fisher RC School, Peterborough

Shall I Compare Thee . . .

Shall I compare thee to a book?
The words fill me with joy,
Once started you pull me in with a hook,
I especially like the character called Roy,
The pictures fill me with haze,
The words inspire me,
People don't know why I daze,
People should just leave me be,
I don't agree with all,
It isn't kind to say stuff like that,
Who needs to know about a fall?
So don't take the mick out of someone's slide - *'kerplat'.*
Overall I think it's great,
It's clearly first rate.

Kelly Smith (13)
St John Fisher RC School, Peterborough

The Dark Is . . .

The Devil's quilt,
The time to sleep,
When children flee the streets,
Inside the coffin,
Living in the forest,
A sheet to cover stars,
The place where vampires lay,
The place where the cats screech,
The place where curses are made,
Colours drained all together,
Nothingness . . .

Laura Epton (13)
St John Fisher RC School, Peterborough

My Love

Shall I compare thee to a daisy?
Your handsome and broad face,
Your tenderness made nicely,
You make my life worthwhile,
All I ask is one special kiss,
And if we're apart by a mile,
That one kiss remains on my lips,
As I stare into your eyes,
And we lie under the stars,
We drown into each other's thoughts,
You hold me tight and tell me your dreams,
And if I die before you do,
While you wonder what to do,
I'll go to Heaven and wait for you.

Elvira Karanja (12)
St John Fisher RC School, Peterborough

The Dark Is . . .

A damp basement
A sense of encasement
A prison cell
A very deep well

Around my head
It's been said
Half the Earth
Before day's birth

A dark cupboard
Empty and closed
A closet with no windows
The dark is Death's cloak.

Ashleigh Harding (13)
St John Fisher RC School, Peterborough

Revenge

The hatred I bear for you,
Is a feeling words cannot say,
For everything you do,
Some day you'll have to pay.
Along will come a knight,
When a smile will shine upon my face,
You'll have to put up a fight,
But you'll lose pace, being such a disgrace.
For you cannot lie,
You'll have to face defeat,
You cannot hide,
You won't succeed.
Your life will have to come to an end,
So be so sweet and lay your head,
For you in this world will be no friend,
Time for you to go to bed.
No one there to take your call,
No one there for your fall.

Sabba Manzer (13)
St John Fisher RC School, Peterborough

The Dark Is . . .

The background of the stage
A toddler's nightmare
Satan's hiding place
A devil's lucky day
Indestructible, unbeatable
Eternally spreading through the world
Like a bottle's hole.

Suraj Singh (13)
St John Fisher RC School, Peterborough

In The Ghetto

What to use in the war today?
The 4-4 or the 4-5, I cannot decide,
Or how about the Uzi or maybe an AK?
I still cannot think, I still cannot decide.
All of them are tucked apart from the glock,
But how about the gat? I still cannot decide.
I must choose quickly before the tick and the tock,
I still cannot choose, I still cannot decide.
A desert eagle or an M-16,
Or maybe a Colt 25? I still cannot decide.
Or even an automatic, so the rest of my team,
I still do not know, I still cannot decide.
The war is over, everyone has died,
I did not choose, I did not get to decide.

Sanchez Thomas (13)
St John Fisher RC School, Peterborough

Shall I . . . ?

Shall I compare thee to Shakespeare?
What? Better not!
You can't rhyme or make things clear,
You read-like-a-r-o-b-o-t,
Shake's wrote more than one poem or play,
His plays are remembered for hundreds of years,
You only have rubbish to say,
Your writing is one of my worst fears,
Shakespeare is famous around the world,
His plays had a range of subjects,
You, however, only talk about having your hair curled,
You write about broken objects,
How very cruel I may seem,
Unlike Shakespeare, you will never gleam!

Sundeep Kaur (13)
St John Fisher RC School, Peterborough

The Itch

Shall I compare you to a black rose
Like the one that falls on the dead man's grave?
No, because for you, the death just grows
That is a sad time, even for the brave.
War, the itch in your mind,
The bodies lay so far away,
But seek and you shall find
That you feel sick today.
Guns are fired, it's your final word,
Your feelings of hate
Blasted upon the world.
After the good threw you some bait.
  The itch of war is a terrible thing,
  Beware, the itch makes others feel the sting.

Josh Allen (13)
St John Fisher RC School, Peterborough

The Fire Animal

Flames flashing across your face like cats' claws.
Listening to the purring as it cuddles and clings to you,
Red, yellow and ginger tom.
Glowing like his eyes in a darkened bush,
And all that is left is its litter buried into the ground.
Reaching and grabbing out for his prey,
Warming your insides from its warm heart.
Climbing up your legs to greet you,
Screeching, longing to sink into you.
Growing taller, growing older, pleasing its master,
All it leaves for you is its heart and ashes.

Laura Black (12)
St John Fisher RC School, Peterborough

Basketball

Basketball is my favourite sport.
I like the way they dribble up and down the court.
The best part about it is the slam dunk,
It's better than that free kick football junk.
If you disagree with me, I don't care,
As long as I am still a basketball player.
The best basketball player in NBA history,
Was Michael Jordan, who won his matches easily.
He won six championships for the Chicago Bulls,
He even thrashed those LA Lakers fools.
Detroit Pistons won the cup last season,
But, oh well, next season the Bulls will beat them.

Zeshaan Butt (13)
St John Fisher RC School, Peterborough

Red Fred!

I once knew a boy named Fred,
Who worshipped a deep shade of red.
He drank scarlet paint,
Then started to faint -
And I should think he's still tucked up in bed!

Eleanor Savill (12)
St John Fisher RC School, Peterborough

Summer Sun

Summer sun
With lots of fun
Loads to do
The sea is blue!

Summer sun
With everything done
Things are great
I made new mates.

The sun is hot
The sea extends
Summer's coming
To its end!

Cassie Barker (13)
Sawston Village College, Sawston

The Cat

On the edge of a sea of green,
There the cat sat all sharp and poised.
Eyes and ears on the alert,
Ready to move at a sudden moment.

Look out, bird,
The coy cat is stalking,
Claws out, ready to pounce.
Too late . . .

The cat sits like a statue,
All satisfied with its prize.
One little lick around the mouth,
The cat disappears.

Imogen Howard (12)
Sawston Village College, Sawston

Just A Reality Away

Descending into subconsciousness . . .
A magical world of impossibilities . . .
Littered with new ideas, thoughts, creations.
A unique new place.

Twisted thoughts spin new worlds.
Emotions roller-coaster new highways.
Unspoken passions expressed in the secrecy of dreamland.
A new reality born.

Thoughts and emotions cross the border to a black land,
Where truth and goodness are corrupted.
Evil monsters sneak uninvited into subconsciousness.
Another reality evolves.

Dreamland begins to fade away.
Screaming silhouettes transform to alarm bells.
New thoughts steal into consciousness.
Reality of waking moments returns.

But which is the true reality?

Victoria Paulding (15)
Sawston Village College, Sawston

Fire

I am hot and angry,
You can't run away from me!

I will burn your homes,
And barbecue your cows.
You can't run away from me.

You will not stop me smoking,
Even if I die.
I will always be here,
But remember, you can't run away from me.

Ryan Judges (13)
Sawston Village College, Sawston

The Poltergeist

Down on Earth lives the poltergeist,
It scares the living with all its might.
It hides behind things when you're coming,
In the dark you hear it humming.

During the night,
It may give you a fright.
Just hold on to your pillow tight,
And pray you sail through the night.

But still do fear,
It's always near,
When you feel a lingering tear.
When you move you're most sincere,
To them it is most certainly clear.

Now I have to say goodnight,
If you find you're in a plight,
Just hold on to that pillow tight,
And hope you make it through the night.

Charley Loveridge (13)
Sawston Village College, Sawston

Cars

Fast and furious
Raging bulls out loose
Wheels like drills tightening screws
Tough and proud
All gather a crowd!

Small, tall
Crawl and brawl
All get you around.

David Rudgley (13)
Sawston Village College, Sawston

Beware Of The School

Beware of the cooks
And their deadly food
Beware of the teachers
Who are always in a mood

Beware of the bullies
Who are ready to fight
Beware of the teachers
And all their might

Beware of the playground
I'll give you a graze
Beware of the school plan
It's a big, big maze

Beware of the toilets
Beware of the smokers
Beware of the druggies
And the provokers

Beware of the Head
Beware of the rules
Beware of the art rooms
And the DT tools.

Adam Leaney (13)
Sawston Village College, Sawston

I'm Scared!

I'm scared of all those different things
Of birds, of bats, of wings
And loads of other things
I don't like herds of huge animals
I don't like deep, deep pools
I don't like big fish swimming in great shoals
I hate life!

Melissa Martin (12)
Sawston Village College, Sawston

They Are Us

They think the world will last forever
They think that life will last forever
They take for granted the things they love
And don't realise they need them until they're gone
When they are younger they want to be older
But when they are older they want to be younger
You can probably guess who they are
As they are us.

Grace Furbank (12)
Sawston Village College, Sawston

Circus

The lions, the monkeys, the camels,
The trucks, the cages, the bars,
The pain the animals go through
All for
The enjoyment of us.
The fire, the lights, the fans,
And the loss of a family,
The kids, the mums, the dads.

Oliver Blackburne-Maze (12)
Sawston Village College, Sawston

Animal Cruelty Poem

Mum, I want to go to the circus, Mum
I want to see the monkeys in their small cages
I want to see the horses in their heavy bridles

Mum, I want to see the lions getting whipped by clowns
I want to see the elephants in their funny dresses
Mum, I don't want to see the circus.

Michael Keelin (11)
Sawston Village College, Sawston

Pain

I'm lost, drowning in this pain.
My world is falling apart without you.
I don't know where to turn,
I'm screaming in my head.
I just can't hold on anymore.

You were my fairy tale, my dream come true,
My first love.
You said I was your world.
You said you'd never leave me.
I thought you weren't like them,
I thought you could never hurt me.

But you wouldn't even tell your friends.
I should have known you'd treat me wrong.
I gave you everything I had;
You took it all,
Left me with nothing.
We were best friends and you broke my heart.

After all we'd been through;
You couldn't even tell me the truth.
So confused, I didn't know what to do.
Hiding behind a breaking smile,
Trying to be strong.
I made the hardest decision of my life then left.
For the last time.

Now I'm still hurting, you don't even look back.
All I see is you and her.
Tell me how you moved on so fast,
How you forgot about me so soon.
Please. I'm trying to forget the past,
Move on with my life and forgive you.

Tears are falling, my heart is empty,
And I still don't understand.
How did I end up like this? Where did I go wrong?
Why did you make me love you?

I hate you but you're all I want.

Natalie Sawcer (15)
Sawston Village College, Sawston

Queen Of The Deep

The sea,
An endless abyss,
Home to many creatures,
But death is hiding, watching,
Waiting, stalker of the sea.
A splash of raging water,
A flash of gleaming teeth,
The fin cuts through the waters,
Like the scythe of death.
A streamlined bullet,
Set to find its mark.
Fish, pray she doesn't find you,
She is the hunter - you are the prey.
A menacing glare from eyes of marble,
Reflecting their owner's shameless sea of slaughter,
The once blue sea dyed red.
But really, just a misjudged creature,
She is gentle at heart,
But rage is coiled in her guts,
A gentle creature - a whiff of blood -
A dangerous psychopath.
Prejudiced, judged, given an unfair trial,
An innocent man to be hanged.
The thrilling tension of her presence,
Could be cut with a baby's rubber spoon.
So not an eating machine,
Not a heartless monster,
The majestic queen of the deep.

Samuel Betz (11)
Sawston Village College, Sawston

Wolf

The moonlit beauty padded along with ease
Power oozed from the silky grey
Her eyes glistened like sparkling diamonds
Deep-set in shadow
The bloodstained killer
Never known
Until it's too late
And then she descends
Swift, strong, silent
Midnight prowler bears scars
Of distant battles
The pain in her ancient eyes
Still remains
In her majestic features
She seats herself
And sings to the lunar
Goddess of darkness.

Pippa Bransfield-Garth (12)
Sawston Village College, Sawston

Dog!

A dog is . . .
Loud barker,
Cat chaser,
Savage eater,
Fierce runner,
Food scavenger,
Long sleeper,
Cuddly creature,
Bone chewer,
And a man's best friend!

Matthew Dockerill (12)
Sawston Village College, Sawston

Unicorn

The majestic and the mystical,
Silent, horned, silver horse,
Staring, golden eyes, glittering, golden horn,
Magical, calm angel,
Here one moment,
Gone the next,
Swift as the light itself,
Leaping into the rainbows,
Over the green, leafy forests,
Purer than pure,
Loving and delicate,
Beautiful queen of the forests.

Dawn Jackson (12)
Sawston Village College, Sawston

Wolves

The emperors of all life,
Eyes like great, golden suns,
Packs more ferocious than the cerberii,
The soft padding of their paws like feathers on ice,
The howling like a banshee,
The bones of the hordes they have devoured,
Teeth like great racks of ivory spears,
Like wraiths they hunt,
Nothing stands in their way.

Tomas Vujakovic (12)
Sawston Village College, Sawston

The Lonely Alien

Flashing, whirring, bright lights all around,
Slowly breathing, not daring to make a sound.
Hidden beneath long corn,
Waiting, hoping they have gone.

Somewhere close by,
A figure catches my eye,
It's as tall as a tree,
And it's God-damn ugly.

It glows against the hanging night air,
I can see it clearly from my shallow lair.
Its black eyes blink,
As it begins to think.

'Meep, meep, meep,'
It begins to speak!
Calling for others,
I start to shudder.

'Meep, meep, meep,'
It repeats,
Over and over,
Echoing all over.

Calling and calling but no one replies,
Tears well up in its massive eyes.
Trickling down its oval face,
Its friends gone without a trace.

It climbs in its ship,
Ready for its trip.
A space reserved for one,
With everyone else gone.

Stacey Pearson (15)
Sawston Village College, Sawston

Along Came A Spider

A lone,
L ight is gone,
O nly dust and darkness,
N othing but shadowy black,
G loom and decay.

C reeping blackness,
A ll is deserted.
M idnight eternal,
E verything consumed.

A time far away.

S omething lives. . .
P utrid,
I solated,
D eadly,
E mpty blackness,
R eminiscent of nightmares.

Abigail Hunt (15)
Sawston Village College, Sawston

Empty

How empty is an empty cup?
As empty as young girl's heart?
A broken heart, a cold heart.
She who feels nothing, nil.
But for those who do,
How empty are they inside?
Desolate? Drained?

Jess Loveday (14)
Sawston Village College, Sawston

You

I know you don't like me
I don't like you
The way you smile
The crease it makes
The spots on your nose
Running up your face
Glasses tumbling down
The roughness of your skin
Like patterned quilt work
Eyes drowning in pools
Of melted chocolate
Sun kisses jumping up and down
Solemn face, rounded chin
Staring at my worst enemy
Finding out
It is me.

Pamela Akita (14)
Sawston Village College, Sawston

Otter

Able-bodied, watchful-eyed,
The swift master of the lake,
Outswims fish in the swirling waters,
Diving from the bank leaving just a ripple on the surface,
Then departing the river to roam on the land,
Rudder-like tail pounding the bank like a hammer,
Glinting claws shining like the midnight stars,
Razor-sharp teeth ripping sparkling fish apart,
Great, sinewed glider cutting through the streams like a knife
through butter,
Sleek, brown-furred king of the deep,
Fast as an arrow, piercing the waves to stab its prey,
Gracefully drifting around on the currents,
The prince of land and water.

Norman Garrick (12)
Sawston Village College, Sawston

The Unicorn

His coat is like snowflakes,
Woven with silk.
When he goes galloping,
He flows like milk.

His nature is all gentle,
His heart very bold,
His single horn magic,
And is worth more than gold.

Nobody rides the unicorn,
As he gazes under the scorching sun,
His understanding is so great,
That he forgives everyone.

Nobody rides the unicorn,
He is the loveliest of them all.
His mind is as peaceful as the swaying grass,
And hides behind the rushing waterfall.

Lisa Chatterton (12)
Sawston Village College, Sawston

Advice To A Teenager

It is a jungle out there,
For teenage problems,
The lions roar,
Like my throbbing temple,
The trees dropping,
When you're down and sad,
The storm high above,
Like a thought in my mind,
The raindrops fall,
Like tears in my eyes,
My body is lifeless,
When I am exhausted and tired.

Megan Ayres (13)
Sawston Village College, Sawston

The Wilderness In Me . . .

There is a squirrel in me, arranging, plumping its nest,
A hoarder,
A fussing, pernickety organiser,
A scurrier, always on the move.

There is a sparrow in me,
A petty squabbler,
A picky, irritating botherer, hopping on a sun-warmed fence,
A merry chatterer of nonsense,
A restless fidgeter, fluttering and calling endlessly.

There is a donkey in me,
A stubborn awkwardness,
A headstrong single-mindedness,
A determined unswayability, tired of being ordered,
I never change my mind.

There is an elephant in me,
A grey shadow on the horizon of a dry landscape,
A slow ponderer,
A quiet thinker,
A plodding dreamer,
Developed a thick skin to ignore and turn away.

There is a dolphin in me,
Splashing, unbothered,
Playful and laid-back,
Happy-go-lucky nostalgia,
Energy for eternity.

I have a wilderness in me,
An evolution from the dawn of time,
A wild soul,
It is me, it is the wilderness.

Ella Gough (12)
Sawston Village College, Sawston

Life On Mars

Beneath your feet
Orange, red, golden
Dust sprinkled on
The rusting rocks
And black-purple shadows
Like bruises on the landscape.

Above your head
Dark, black sky
Host to a million lights
Dancing across the darkness
In the day
Red suns
Drifting across
Orange skies
Like a child's balloon
Lost and floating in the sky.

It is the Red Planet
Fourth from the sun
  My home
    Mars.

Jade Field (13)
Sawston Village College, Sawston

Cats

C ute, cuddly creatures.
A ttacking annoying animals.
T erritorial, tiny tigers.
S ly, sleek, sneaky.

Jessica Holder (12)
Sawston Village College, Sawston

Shark

A solitary fin, the first sign of danger,
Darting through the waves,
Seeking the distorted, billowing blood of prey,
It blindly slashes out,
Viciously cutting through flesh and bone,
The legendary image of ocean death,
Humans, fish or swimming mammals -
All victims of this remorseless demon,
It shows no emotion, no feelings behind its dead eyes,
Never blinks, never misses a moment,
Stealth and crazy bloodshed mingle together in its sleek bullet
                                                        of a body,
An almost visible aura of evil surrounds it,
The splash of disturbed water is its roar,
Alone, but deadly.

Beni Bienz (12)
Sawston Village College, Sawston

Football Be Fun

There once was a fellow called Paul
Who was no use at soccer at all
He kicked his own striker
Three dogs and a biker
The only thing safe was the ball.

Tom Spicer (11)
Sawston Village College, Sawston

Jungle Cat

Running towards
The smell
Quickly moving
Steadily slowing.

Prey in sight
Moving jiggly
Gathering food
For its family.

Slowly creeping about
Its prey
Grass blades moving
Frightfully away.

Breathing steadily
Claws ready
Pounce positioned
Gulp!

Emma-Jane Elsom (13)
Sawston Village College, Sawston

Life

Life can be:

L ovely
I ncredible
F antastic
E xciting

But it can be:

L oathsome
I mpenetrable
F earful
E xcruciating.

Toni Pateman (13)
Sawston Village College, Sawston

The Night Performance

The curtains are lifted and a great secret is whispered into the
watching ears.
The show has begun.
The spotlight looms high in the sky, casting its rays of light
across the stage.
And the maracas start playing, swaying, shaking.
Ripples of sound falling softly to the ground.
The flute perched in a tree takes its cue and plays a soft melody
to the drumming of the rain.
Tu-whit tu-whoo, tu-whit tu-whoo, tu-whit tu-whoo . . .

And at this point the puppet master is sitting high up,
gazing down at the stage,
Unseen by the audience but playing the main part in this show.
He lifts his hand and the strings dance obediently,
answering to his call.

Two figures appear on the stage.
An unrehearsed chase breaks out.
The drumming beat races, *dum, dum, dum*
and the maracas quake in fear.
A shrill scream pierces the air and the onlookers gasp in horror.
The two actors scatter across the floor in a manic attempt
to save the show.
Too late . . . the prey has fallen and is lost.
The dominant creature snarls and devours the spotlight.

The puppet master drops the strings and lets his figures rest,
Without moving he poisons the flute, strangles the scream,
and stabs the drumming sound in its beating heart.
The spotlight dims and the curtains are closed.

Then, without them noticing,
he takes the audience by their strings
and lets the curtains open onto a play
where he is the only spectator.

Fionnuala Kavanagh (13)
Sawston Village College, Sawston

To A Baboon From A Human

Your itchy armpits,
Your bright blue bums,
Your squashed-in noses,
And your rumbly tums,
Your hairy toes,
Your scratchy fleas,
Your waddling movement,
And your buckled knees,
Your love for bananas,
You must feel sick,
Your fighting is brave,
But you've got to be quick,
How can you stand all those things?
But I suppose that's what life brings.

The baboon answers back:

Your slimy, shaved armpits,
Your pink, podgy bums,
Your stuck-up noses,
And your squidged-in tums,
Your pointy toes,
You've got no fleas,
Your sharp, jagged movement,
And your straight-up knees,
Your icky, sticky food,
You must feel sick,
You're not at all brave,
But you are pretty quick,
How can you stand all those things?
But I suppose that's what life brings.

Hannah Muncey (12)
Sawston Village College, Sawston

The Tiger

The tiger roams the jungle
His paws padding along the ground
When its tummy begins to rumble
Looking for food he has not yet found

He senses that food is near
He follows his scent along the floor
And in the distance he spots a deer
And he's getting hungry more and more

He creeps up on his prey
His vivid stripes glinting in the sun
Giving him camouflage to hide away
He then leaps up and starts to run

His claws and teeth are as sharp as glass
And he intends to dig them into the deer
But to do that he has to move fast
He does just that and catches his meal.

Sam Fleck (12)
Sawston Village College, Sawston

A Toddler's World

Our world is a fantasy world
Full of magic tricks and treats.
With our wings and wands
To our cloaks and swords, we'd
Be someone different each week.
From a cardboard box to the big
Outdoors we'd have an adventure
Either way,
Because our world is a fantasy
World and we always have
Something to play.

Pippa Boagey (13)
Sawston Village College, Sawston

Is This The World We Created?

Is this the world we created?
We've made it all our own.
Is this the world we devastated
Right through to the bone?
If there's a God
In the sky,
Looking down,
What must He think of
What we've done
To the world that He created?

Is this the world we created?
What did we do it for?
Is the world we created
Against the law?
The damage is done,
The effects are everlasting.
It is now gone
The world that we created.

Dominic Vickers (14)
Sawston Village College, Sawston

If I Was . . .

If I was a big oak tree,
I'd live for a 100 years, I'd be free.
If I was a big oak tree,
I'd grow lots of leaves and sway in the breeze.
If I was a big oak tree,
I'd grow big and tall, I'd have no worries about weeds.
This is what it would be like to be an oak tree.

Amy Saggers (14)
Sawston Village College, Sawston

London's Hour

London's hour of despair
Innocent lives lost
This life is not fair
Tearful eyes
Blackened, darkened skies
Prayers were spoken
Hearts were broken
London's hour of despair.

London's hour of death and pain
Will there be peace after the rain?
Commuters boarding an underground train
Terrorists' brutal violence
Dreaded silence
Bloodshed
Over forty dead
Another day that shook the world
London's hour of death and pain.

Jamie Page (14)
Sawston Village College, Sawston

Emotions

I lie nervous,
Feeling what's inside,
No one around,
Crying,
Never pretending,
The truth comes,
My mind full,
On the outside,
Happy,
Sad,
Scared,
Worried,
All in one,
Emotions.

Nicola Slater (14)
Sawston Village College, Sawston

The Loony Dalek

Exterminate, exterminate,
Zap, zap, zap!
Disintegrating homework in a thunderclap!
The children thank him kindly,
Then go out and play,
Enjoying all the benefits of a lovely summer's day.
He takes the disabled,
Across the road and to the beach,
And extends his arm in shops to get things they can't reach.

You may wonder why 'loony',
Is his official state of mind,
When all he's really doing,
Is being really kind.
Well, let me ask a question,
Just one thing I ask you,
Is this what you would expect,
Normal Daleks to do?

Kit Westlake (14)
Sawston Village College, Sawston

Zinc

Zinc is something rather funny
Especially when it's in your tummy
You'll squirm and slither
Come over in a shiver
What a shame zinc isn't honey.

Chris Ould (14)
Sawston Village College, Sawston

It's What's Inside That Counts!

Fashion, fashion
It's everywhere
Why does it matter?
Is it really that important?
Discrimination against everyone
Chavs
Goths
Tarts
Grebs!
Isn't it what's inside that counts?

Nothing matters
Nothing like
Does my bum look big in this?
Am I too short?
Am I too tall?
Am I too fat?
Am I too skinny?
My skin isn't perfect!
Isn't it what's inside that counts?

We've all got a heart
Behind the slap
Behind the discrimination
Behind what others think
Everyone's perfect in their own way
No one needs to change
So live life to the maximum!
Enjoy yourself, because
It's what's inside that counts!

Rosie Tasker (14)
Sawston Village College, Sawston

Cancer!

I can remember when I first heard your name
Cancer
I repeated it over in my head
Cancer
What did you mean?
What do you do?
Why did you come?
Everything changed

I asked my friends
No one knew
But then I saw
I saw the destruction you brought
The pain
The heartbreak
No one smiled
Everything changed

Everything changed
I've seen your power
Your dark shadow
Forever on our lives
Loved ones gone
Why?
Why us?
I can remember when I first heard your name.

Alice Tasker (14)
Sawston Village College, Sawston

Believe

Satanic sand sieving roughly on my withered feet,
The sun rising rapidly, like God majestically awakening,
I fall hard to my knees, quivering.

He keenly brandishes it, beating me, like savage trinity,
Persevere, I shall.

A white dove soars lovingly through the air,
Looking down on me.

I will not be blinded like Isaac,
I must carry on,
I must believe.

Charlotte Levien (14)
Sawston Village College, Sawston

The Phoenix

Smoke,
Fire,
Burning forest,
Life destroyed,
Everything lost,
Suddenly a spark,
Rising and twisting,
Shoots up the fiery phoenix,
Wings of gold flame,
Flying like a comet,
Light shines down upon the ruins,
And slowly life returns.

Stuart Chamley (14)
Sawston Village College, Sawston

Poverty In Africa

Young children gasp for air,
Shivering with cold,
Curled up together,
Bones like piercing sticks.
Think!
We hog our money,
Infinite greed,
Pennies that Africa needs.
Water shortage,
Throats of dying children dry up!
Diseases crumble organs of life.
Think!
Make poverty history!

Laura Waller (14)
Sawston Village College, Sawston

What Am I?

I'm big or small
Depending on you
I overhang like an umbrella
Always here whatever the weather
I am a part of nature
So my colour you can guess
My raindrops drip off me
But my body still stands strong.
What am I?

Sophie Lloyd (14)
Sawston Village College, Sawston

Unjust Love

I don't know what happened,
But it hurts so much in my head,
My side is numb and I'm so weak,
God, I feel like I'm dead.

My eyes are glued shut,
And I can't feel my hand,
I think my leg's bleeding,
But I'm unable to stand.

Now I'm starting to panic,
My heart's beating too fast,
What's going on?
How come I'm seeing the past?

I feel better now,
I feel so light and free,
My eyes are open now,
I can finally see!

But nothing looks or feels right,
I'm seeing you from above,
You're looking and laughing at me,
Is this really your love?

Now I see what's happened,
I remember it all,
Your love was so kind,
But then it turned so cruel.

Your face is twisted and bloody,
You're full of anger and hate,
What did I do to deserve this?
I want to say sorry but it's too late.

But I guess I'm going to be happy up above,
I'm free from you and your unkind love!

Hannah Miller (15)
Sir Charles Lucas Arts College, Colchester

Witch Burning

My daughter,
Accused,
Blast it all,
My beautiful girl,
When all this time . . .

They found the chicken legs,
They found the magic stones,
They pointed a finger,
And said, 'Witch!'

My daughter,
Accused,
Blast it all,
My beautiful girl,
When all this time . . .

They tied her to a stake,
They set fire to the hay,
They pointed a finger,
And said, 'Die!'

My daughter,
Accused,
Blast it all,
My beautiful girl,
When all this time - I am the witch!

Michael Johnston (14)
Sir Charles Lucas Arts College, Colchester

It's Autumn

In the autumn time,
The trees shed their leaves as they get ready to sleep.
Small animals start to hibernate and lie in the leaves.
Ants will die out and the queen will be left,
While the fir trees will grow and turn white in the winter snow.
When the air turns too cold and the rains start to fall,
Puddles will form ice and the roads will over-freeze.

Matthew Robinson (13)
Sir Charles Lucas Arts College, Colchester

Don't Ever Forget Me

A flower may die,
The sun may set,
But a friend like you I can never forget,
Your name is so precious,
It will never grow old,
It's engraved in my heart,
In letters of gold!

Someone, somewhere dreams of your smile,
And while thinking of you, says life is worthwhile,
So when you're lonely,
Remember it's true,
Someone, somewhere is thinking of you!

Rebecca Osborne (13)
Sir Charles Lucas Arts College, Colchester

Grandad, Now You're Gone

(In memory of Mr R Moorcroft: 25th May 1932 - 1st October 2004)

I love you lots
Just looking above at night, you are one of those glowing dots
I know you will cure my fears
Which you can see in my tears
I love you more than I could say
Even now, to this day
I love you so
From my head to my toe
Now you're in a grave
Only if I was there, your life I could have saved.

Ashley Moorcroft (12)
Sir Charles Lucas Arts College, Colchester

A Figure Of Misfortune

An owl's cry squeaks and echoes,
The aging trees sigh at me,
Millions of stars stare as I look up,
So it seems I'm not alone.

The wind squeals as I recite the past,
It's twisting the roots of my mind,
What did I do wrong?
There are no truths to be heard.

I am surrounded by danger,
Every corner hides a new threat,
And I shan't bother to prove my innocence,
Their ears are shut and eyes are bruised.

So I run to the desolate remains of a vast city,
The cold night remains quiet as I trespass,
Lights flitting conspicuously from the lamps in the streets,
Their glow casts haunting shadows along my path.

The bell resounds and the populace awakes,
Their movements strike daggers into my confused mind,
I am in a maze with moving walls,
Their eyes are open but they do not see.

Michael Chau (15)
Sir Charles Lucas Arts College, Colchester

Why?

Why do we cry
Those tears that never dry?
The things that haunt us
To some it's too much of a fuss.
Many today never remember
The pain that those feel forever.
Why do we ponder why?
To this we sigh.

Suraj Rai (14)
Sir Charles Lucas Arts College, Colchester

A Poem About Someone Special

From the beginning to the end
Everyone was her friend

She lost her hair
She didn't care

Chemo made her tired and sick
But through all her treatments she was a strong as a brick

Nan, other family members and friends all played a part in this
Most people helped by giving her support and a kiss

She had breast cancer
She is my mum
I love her no matter what happens
That's why I am lucky and proud to be her son.

Robert Taylor (12)
Sir Charles Lucas Arts College, Colchester

Delicious Chocolate

Feel the creamy, scrumptious chocolate on your tongue.
Taste it melted and creamy and crumbly.
Imagine it sticking to your teeth!
The sensation of the gooey, luscious chocolate
All around your mouth.
The taste, the sensation
   Going,
      Going,
         Gone!

Katrina Smith (12)
Sir Charles Lucas Arts College, Colchester

The Truth About School

What do teachers do at the weekend?
I bet they have wild parties, or go shopping and spend,
Or they come into school, sleep over and mark all our work,
Or get drunk at the pub, as one of life's perks.
Sometimes I wonder if they really have a life,
Or just act all disgustingly loved-up with their husband or wife,
Perhaps they go out and meet all their friends,
Nah, they just do all boring stuff at the weekends.

What do you think teachers shouldn't do?
If they see us eating, don't make us stop but carry on and chew,
Don't give out detentions for no apparent reason,
Or make us wear school uniform in the hot season.
In fact, imagine if they just didn't teach,
I could go on holiday and lay on the beach,
It's because of school that life is 'poo',
And these are just some things that teachers shouldn't do.

Just think about if we never had to go to school,
I would eat ice cream and go swimming in the pool,
I would play my PlayStation and never change me socks,
Watch TV whilst I'm eating Coco Pops.

I would wind up my parents and teach them how to be cool,
Play hide-and-seek and break all the rules,
Annoy my brother and sister when they act like a fool,
I can't wait until the day I don't have to go to school.

Empress Davis (17)
Sir John Lawes School, Harpenden

Poetry Comp

'We are entering a Poetry Comp'
Bet you the winner won't be from this dump
'You may consider this a waste of time'
And yet none of the judges will pick mine
'This is a chance to express one's self'
My entry will gather dust on the shelf
'You are against the whole of the state'
B******s! The winner will be the judge's mate.

'Winning this will bring honour and fame'
The judges report 'this effort was lame'
'The school expects someone in the top ten'
No chance of that living in Harpenden.

'Finally, we encourage you all to learn'
Poetry Comp, a contradiction in terms.

Stuart Brill (17)
Sir John Lawes School, Harpenden

Outside

Don't underestimate my size,
My strength will hold your lives,
Seen and hidden; I am everywhere.

What am I?

I'm soft but you can't feel me,
I'm high and you can reach me,
I'm beautiful far away but disappear when you're near,
Sometimes I make you happy,
Other times I make you sad.

What am I?

Laura Moran (17)
Sir John Lawes School, Harpenden

War Angel

Angel, angel, up above
Come now, save me from all this blood
Free me from this torture and crime
Before we end up crossing the line

Take me from this hellhole site
Reunite me with my family and stop all this fright
No man should suffer such pain
When in the end we will just become insane

Let all the dead soldiers lie
Take me now up to the sky
Let there be peace
Or some justice at least.

Emma Long (17)
Sir John Lawes School, Harpenden

Robin Hood

The thing that I love about Robin Hood,
Is that he is always good.
He steals from the rich to give to the poor,
Just barely escaping from the law.
If ever he were to be caught,
Maid Marion would be so fraught.
But never fear as Robin Hood,
Can forever hide in Sherwood.

Kirsty Maple (17)
Sir John Lawes School, Harpenden

Death

Death is being flung out of reach
Being washed up on some lonely beach
People you left behind do mourn
But you're out of reach, you have gone

A funeral service being prepared for you
Prayers are said behind a pew
Though you miss home you're free to fly
Free, far above Earth, in the sky

You have left life far below
The river of life carries on to flow
Down the river, through the sea
There I'll find you waiting for me

Life is the start of something new
Like the grass with fresh morning dew
You don't know what waits ahead
But to the future you are led

If death is black then life is white
Something special like the candlelight
That shines brightly in the dark
You have walked the Earth and made your mark

You have to live and then to die
It doesn't really matter why
You have to leave this Earth at some time
And there you will find Heaven waiting in the sky.

Abi Banczyk-Sturgeon (12)
Sir John Lawes School, Harpenden

July 7th - Kings Cross

Smoke
Thick and black floods the capsule
Lungs strain to reach the little pure that remains
At first, curiosity
Then realisation
The screaming and panic begins
Leaving little hope of keeping order
A mad rush for the exits;
Continuous smashing of windows;
Crying of the little and the old
All means of escape barred with bodies
Bloody bodies
Whispers of prayer are not heard amongst the terrified riot
Questions . . . Why? Who? How?
And then it's clear.

Claire Hewitt (14)
Sir John Lawes School, Harpenden

A Remembrance

I like to walk through peaceful fields
Once of horrors where dead men keeled
Seeing nothing but the peaceful joys
That were not shared by conscripted boys

Treading softly through the broken clay
Unaware of the dead that lay
Beneath my feet so quiet and dry
The cream of youth employed to die

One hundred years on and nothing's changed
More innocent lives are yet to be claimed
By lying leaders and foolish scum
Who cannot see what war has done.

Ollie Widdowson (17)
Sir John Lawes School, Harpenden

Music

Music, I think, is one of the best things ever
Rock, pop, rap, R 'n' B
Urban, dance, jazz - whatever
Music entertains people
And without it life would be quiet, sad
If it did ever die
You'd be sure to miss the music you had

I love playing music
As well as listening to it
And I always find it great
To hear the greatest hits
But songs also give a message
So a song can sometimes teach
Some songs contain a story
Told by words with rhythmic beat
Music can create memories
And remind people of years ago
It might even leave . . . a memory for tomorrow

So when you listen to music - listen carefully to the rhymes
Some songs make people smile
Others might make you cry
But these emotions can only be found in songs
If you genuinely try
Listen to the words and instruments
And try to look for a meaning
Read between the lines, and maybe
Discover a different musical feeling.

Gwen Jing (12)
Sir John Lawes School, Harpenden

Block

I never thought it would happen.
But it has. I can't believe it.
I've got writer's block.
Before, I could write about anything:
The sun in the sky, the birds in the trees,
The mud on your shoes.

Sometimes I dreamed, and woke to write of revolutions
In imaginary, faraway places.
Fighting against the persistence of memory,
Time, and the person knocking at the door.
Xanadu. Kubla Khan. Coleridge.
I would dream of a never-ending tomorrow
Which would bring endless possibilities
And the fruits to harvest for my future.
A land which is always fertile.
My furrow. My crop.

But now, I cannot write about anything.
I get the feeling that I have lost something:
That I was blessed once by a muse,
Infinitely beautiful and dead to mine ears.
The harp is her instrument, soft so that few can hear;
It is heard with the force of the trumpet by those who dare
To listen.

We had a brief love affair. Passionate, with fire.
But now she is gone, and I feel slightly empty.
An empty, white desert without even bones to
See what remains of what was there.
Now I have
Nothing. Full stop.

Jonathan Rowland (17)
Sir John Lawes School, Harpenden

I Saw . . .

I saw a tiger, creative and fun,
I saw an iguana eating a bun,
I saw a sheep walking on the moon,
I saw a frog which woke in the noon.

I saw a chocolate's empty box,
I saw a spider wearing socks,
I saw a video player full with candles,
I saw a pair of shoes with handles.

I saw a picture floating in the air,
I saw a policeman with no care,
I saw a glass full with a shoe,
I saw a panda using glue.

I saw a bill as big as a shirt,
I saw a bird wearing a skirt,
I saw a pot with a dog inside,
I saw a cube riding a slide.

I saw a flower fearing storm,
I saw a cloud, nice and warm,
I saw home from above,
I saw a scary thing with love.

I saw a man with a baby in his tum,
I saw a mum showing her bum,
I saw a cat saying *bling, bling*,
I saw a monkey shaking its thing.

Yasmin Coot (12)
Sir John Lawes School, Harpenden

I'm Hungry

I am a fast creature
Running through the jungle
As I run

    Through
I get caught

In the
    Muddle

I can't get out

What shall I do?

I try to call

But I begin to
               F
                  A
                     L
                        L
                                    I stop

And I call some more
No one comes
But I am hungry
I could eat a boar.

Sara Ledbury (13)
Sir John Lawes School, Harpenden

Seeing Blind

I saw a fairy, she was filled with love
I saw an angel, its wings as white as a dove
I saw a flower, blooming in the sky
I saw a heart . . . about to die.

Ashleigh Pinchen (12)
Sir John Lawes School, Harpenden

Glory Glory Be To A Chocolate - From The Devil's Pulpit

Created in the mouth of Hell, where the devils dwell
The greatest sin
So I say it twice glory, glory -

An explosion on the taste bud bell
A craving within
Brownies, candies, cookies

A tongue that twinkles
A wrapper which crinkles
Hyperactive, flavoured imps

The happy food
The addiction you can't win
If you choose to fight

The eternal forest
The divine cocoa-erratic pod

Can every mouth taste this god?

Sam Chapple (17)
Sir John Lawes School, Harpenden

Riddle

Standing strong, obeying them,
Automatic and manual,
Opaque or transparent,
I close with a click,
Into the space that is for them to pass through,
Locks are not obligatory,
To separate wide open spaces,
But are to protect.

Door.

Charlotte Roberts (17)
Sir John Lawes School, Harpenden

You'll Never Know

(In the style of Philip Larkin)

Time's path rolls into one
As you stare up
At a fading sun.

Catch a last sigh
And suppress that strong urge
To cry, out loud

In pain - or relief?

So excuse me whilst I kiss the sky
And leave you queasy soldiers
With thoughts of how you'll die.

*'His life became fantastically lit
As he fell towards a hero's glory'*

But don't believe any of it -

For you'll never know
The dark, parting continual, far-out glow.
And you'll never know
How the grey clouds roll into one

Until you stare up and close your eyes
On the fading young.

Chris Mourant (16)
Sir John Lawes School, Harpenden

Nonsense Food

I ate a chocolate that was mouldy green,
I ate a bird that kept me keen,
I ate a pig that was flying in the sky,
I ate an egg that was passing by,
I ate a pea that looked like a rat,
After all that, I'm feeling a bit fat!

Kathryn Hale (14)
Sir John Lawes School, Harpenden

Today

Apathy preached with silent words,
Behind cool screens of static that continue, regardless.
When we all go to die, how long do we sit for?

As one, crowded, stands beside himself; thinking.
There wasn't much, but at least there was some.
A little left, between the great and the good
And the low and the lean.

'The meek shall inherit the Earth!'

Without what was before, what is now?
A momentary lull, the individual paramount.
Substance of us, the past, the pit.
Wheels cease to turn.

'Open yourselves up to us.'

While the cogs of elsewhere grind forward,
With unrelenting speed, a need?
Remove the seventh twice over, then add by half again.
And you'd be right, my friend.

Martin Nickolay-Blake (17)
Sir John Lawes School, Harpenden

Sir John Lawes

Six years have passed and I'm still here,
Flowing down the river of my education career.
Through the rain, fog, snow and sun I come,
Which can be up and down in terms of fun.
Teachers nagging at every wrong,
Just keep yourself low until they're gone.
Laughing about the common room far from hurt,
Prodded by Mrs Barrett to do some *work!*
Looking forward to my final year
At a school which has brought me tears, laughter,
And a place of memories.

Ashley Smith (17)
Sir John Lawes School, Harpenden

The Pretend Rifle

Eight men in fettered khaki suits
A business day of sorts . . .
Each man with dreamy, lustless eyes
And mud-stained British shorts

'I hurt; I hurt . . . my dying eyes'
A lover incandescent dress
The soldiers far away from home
A mother in distress

He fell to ochre ground; his heaving, gasping sigh
His death and life that left him there
Beneath a dark French sky

Pretend rifles slung, unslung
Like false toy pretends
A smoking gunshot enter wound, another heartfelt death
By day we hear the salient guns' breath like ice vapour duress
Like mist and smoke and kiss goodbyes.

Each man, each man . . . they fall and die.

Owen Vince (17)
Sir John Lawes School, Harpenden

Just Imagine

I saw a dog made of sparkling glass
I saw a bird eating grass
I saw a cow biting a bone
I saw a window all alone.

Vanessa Wedd (12)
Sir John Lawes School, Harpenden

Tom Heal's Nonsense Day

I saw a swimming pool eating loads of trash,
I saw a puppy dog making a big splash,
I saw a teacher biting someone's leg,
I saw a bunny rabbit tied up with a peg,
I saw a rich man hopping down a hill,
I saw an elephant paying for the bill,
I saw a lady scratching on a tree,
I saw a monkey sipping down some tea,
I saw a blue car running up a lamp post,
I saw a dustbin squishing some burnt toast.

Tom Heal (13)
Sir John Lawes School, Harpenden

Until Now

I have never been hurt before,
This cut still runs deep.
Deep through my veins,
Until I am crying out in pain.

I cannot forget it.
Cannot move on.
What can I do to forget you?

Lauren Weller (13)
Sir John Lawes School, Harpenden

My Nonsense Poem

I saw a pig with no head
I saw a plane, it was trying to fly
I saw a man in the sky
I saw a pigeon which was lying dead.

Harry Gough (12)
Sir John Lawes School, Harpenden

The Raven

The raven is the bird of death
Its dark cry fills the night
Wherever it flies there is shadow
And kindness becomes hatred

The raven is the reaper's pet
The servant of bad luck
It wants to cause destruction
And make war between nations

Its black feathers are like burnt sticks
And its eyes are cold and evil
Its tongue feeds on the dead
Its mind is filled with darkness

The raven is from the abyss
An escaped demon from Hell
It is a sign of gloom
And a curse to all mortals

The raven will never be stopped
It is the unresting spirit
It wishes to end the life of light
And bring shade to the world.

Travis Clausen-Knight (14)
The Arts Educational School, Tring

King Of The Mountain

Swooping and gliding
Around the mountain
In the most graceful manner
Is an eagle
The true king of the mountain.

His golden plumage
Rippling in the cool breeze
Like the velvet cloak of royalty
Which makes him
The most regal of the mountain.

His sharp eyes and
Keen intellect
Mixed with his long talons and ripping beak
Making him
The top predator of the mountain.

He sees a treacherous hare
Small and quick
With the speed of a bullet
He dives
The fastest of the mountain.

His long talons close around
The helpless hare
And he glides back to his rocky outcrop
To eat his royal banquet
This beast is the king of the mountain.

Sam Bishop
The Arts Educational School, Tring

The Penguin

3 . . . 2 . . . 1 . . . The penguin slides . . .
Off the ice and into the sea,
Searching for some food.
Swimming like a torpedo,
In its nice and smart tuxedo.

3 . . . 2 . . . 1 . . . Then suddenly . . .
A blizzard comes,
The penguins huddle close together,
Sharing each others' heat,
Warming the babies on their feet.

3 . . . 2 . . . 1 . . . Through the waves . . .
His sharp strokes help him
Catch a fish, he feeds
His family just one fish,
Makes a charming, lovely dish.

3 . . . 2 . . .1 . . . In the pitch-black . . .
Of night, the penguins
Stroll upon the ice.
Penguins black and white as cats
In tailcoats and tall top hats!

Harriet van der Vliet (14)
The Arts Educational School, Tring

An Ode To The Snake

Sliding through realms,
Eve's tempter curls as withered ivy does,
Is he aware of his feared throne?
Bible's stabbing words gave him his place,
Snake lives in a
Veiled world,
Subtle, gentle, beautiful.
Merging with ground,
He leaves a trail in the soft sand.

Camilla Ker (13)
The Arts Educational School, Tring

The Red Squirrel

He stands on his hind legs,
Sniffing the air,
Then scurries off like a mouse,
To his home - who knows where.

He springs like an athlete,
From the treetops,
This squirrel is a gymnast,
That never ever stops.

He grasps his acorn,
With human-like paws.
At first he nibbles slowly,
Then like a tiger he gnaws.

He is small and timid,
With a fiery tail,
With beady little eyes,
Tiptoes across a fence rail.

At night he sits,
Like a cat at home,
And lies there lazily,
As still as a garden gnome.

Rachel Griggs (14)
The Arts Educational School, Tring

Thunder And Lightning - Haiku

Thunder and lightning
The sky's veins bleeding on Earth
Crashing down on us.

Adam Blanchette (12)
The Colne Community School, Brightlingsea

Teenage Life

It's difficult being at my age,
Life's so hard and testing,
Parents keep you locked in a cage,
And are constantly pestering.

From Mum it's, 'Don't do this.'
From Dad it's, 'Don't do that.'
From friends it's, 'Who did you kiss?'
And from me it's, 'Why am I so fat?'

Sometimes I look upon a path,
To see what I can find,
Someone to make me giggle and laugh,
Someone who is always kind.

But at my age that just doesn't happen,
People run away,
At school you feel low and dampened,
Until school has ended for the day.

So teenage life is not so great,
When you're lonely and unhappy,
I suppose I will have to wait,
Until the day that I am happy.

Kara Worsley (13)
The Colne Community School, Brightlingsea

Last Minute Equaliser

The crowd roar,
As the players score,
The keeper dives to save his life,
The ref blows as players moan,
1-0 down and we're going home,
90th minute, need to score
All of a sudden there comes a roar,
A shot on goal, to the net,
Never shall we ever forget!

James Booth (12)
The Colne Community School, Brightlingsea

Disaster

I met Disaster
Last week on the tube
He hit me quickly
I didn't know what to do.

He flashed, he smiled
No, he destroyed!
The tube came to a halt
I began to cry.

He knocked people out
With a punch of his fist.
The train began to rock.
How could he do this?

He grazed people's faces,
Broke people's hands.
Shocked innocent people
And made children cry.

Disaster glared at me,
A grin on his face.
He began to step
Further and further away.

I climbed through the rubble,
Clambering past the dead,
Through the dark tunnel
To safety light ahead.

Why did Disaster
Do this to me?
I saw him earlier today
Wrecking many lives.

Hannah Moss
The Colne Community School, Brightlingsea

Teenage Poem

When parents break up it's a nightmare
Makes you realise how life is unfair.

Happens to a lot of people
Makes me lose a lot of sleep.

Divorce bills, papers and settlements too
Even your parents don't know what to do.

They just want this all to end
Oh look! Another bill has just been sent.

Hearts are broken, lives destroyed
Worse than that it really annoys.

Then along comes the stepdad and stepmum
Man, I wish I had a gun!

Soon after that everyone's engaged, will they never learn?
The end . . . or is it the beginning?

Henry Sheales (12)
The Colne Community School, Brightlingsea

Teenage Poem

I am a teenage boy
I'd like a big toy
It's called a motorbike
There's a lot more I'd like
But a motorbike I'd like the most
Another thing I'd like
Is a nice mountain bike
One with good suspension
Then I'd get a lot of attention
When I go over the jumps
And do lots of stunts
When you're a teenager you
Want everything.

Joe Bowes (13)
The Colne Community School, Brightlingsea

A Girl Caught Out

A girl in my class spreads lots of rumours,
Giant lies get spread about,
I think her heart is full of nonsense,
Remembering lies and swearing,
Lessons are the least important to her when she has to learn.

I see her swear at people and get sent out,
Never on time to lessons.

Maybe she just likes doing laps for no reason,
You can see her walking around the school over and over.

Curiously the teacher asks, 'Why are you so late?'
'Last lesson was boring
And the teacher caught me snoring
So I had to do twenty laps of the school!'
'So obvious you're lying, detention for you,
    You got caught!' the teacher shouted.

Tiffany Spong (13)
The Colne Community School, Brightlingsea

Growing Pains

Sometimes it's fun
Sometimes it's sad
Sometimes for no reason, you get really mad
You have loads of arguments
With your mum and dad
Arguments you've already had
Sometimes about money
Sometimes about school
Or about leaving something in your neighbour's swimming pool
Weird things start happening
I'd rather not explain
I wake in the night with terrible growing pains
But in the end, teenage life's alright
Even if I still have sleepless nights.

Jacob Harding (14)
The Colne Community School, Brightlingsea

London Explosion!

Suddenly a light flared up brighter than the sun,
For the moment I was blinded,
I could hear only screams and shouts,
I could see soot-covered faces dead and alive.

The pain seared through me like a blazing fire,
Feeling warm blood trickling down my face,
I smashed the nearest window
And climbed into the foreboding tunnel.

The smoke and heat near unbearable,
I scrambled over all,
Dead people, debris and the tracks,
As I neared the exit,
The wind swept over me like a blanket of water.

Now, looking back at that explosion,
It feels like a flame that burns me from within,
Like a curse that haunts me in my dreams,
And like an itch under my bare skin.

Bryony Bull (12)
The Colne Community School, Brightlingsea

Fairies

They glisten in the sunlight,
Colours dancing in the room,
Whisper, laughter, flopping, bright,
They brighten up the gloom.

My friends are very special,
They come but once a year,
No one else believes me,
That the fairies are still here!

Madeleine Ward (12)
The Colne Community School, Brightlingsea

The Girl No More

She never saw,
She was never seen.
There was so hope,
There was only dreams.
Never was a day,
She went out and about.
Only was the night,
That she stepped out.

But once came a man,
That knocked on her door.
She sat in silence,
Curled up on the floor.
Her curtains shut,
No light peering in.
The unusual visitor,
Wanting to come in.

Night fell once more,
And she opened her door.
Stood standing outside,
Was the man as before.
She ran down the street,
In hope not to meet.
Only to find,
The man was behind.

She stopped and stood still,
Looking ready to kill.
The man came up close,
He saw only her ghost.
As her body faded,
She was no more,
Than the dark girl,
Who hid behind the door.

Beth Wallis (14)
The Colne Community School, Brightlingsea

Oldest To Youngest

When we were at primary school,
We were the oldest,
We were the height of cool,
But now we're the youngest,
And we have no privileges at all.

It wasn't easy being older,
We had to do everything right,
But we were braver and bolder,
We were the tallest in sight.

It's OK being youngest,
Teachers make allowances,
Older people thinking they're the best,
You get given more chances.

Even though we are younger,
We are still just as cool!

Stephanie Collins (12)
The Colne Community School, Brightlingsea

Burning Bright - Haikus

Fire
Fire, fire, burning bright,
The cat's tail was set alight,
Fire, fire, burning bright.

Thunder
The thunder rumbled,
Lightning lit up the black sky,
The house exploded.

Depths of darkness
In depths of darkness,
The creature stirred and awoke,
To release its wrath.

Nathan Carlisle (13)
The Colne Community School, Brightlingsea

Haiku

A night as black as
Ebony, a dress as red
As the reddest rose.

Jacqueline Bushnell-Lledó (12)
The Colne Community School, Brightlingsea

Hungry? - Haiku

Smooth, lovely, scrummy,
Sweet, creamy, ever so nice,
I love chocolate!

Mary Beadles (12)
The Colne Community School, Brightlingsea

Deserted - Haiku

Cold, wintry mountain
Dead bushes blowing around
A miserable day.

Myles Blackwell (12)
The Colne Community School, Brightlingsea

Goal - Haiku

He collects the ball,
He does one then another,
Rifles a shot, goal!

Steven Green (12)
The Colne Community School, Brightlingsea

Penguins - Haiku

Dots of black and white
Nothing but penguins for miles
Ice is all around.

Rosie Kippen (12)
The Colne Community School, Brightlingsea

The Forest - Haiku

Crispy, yellow leaves
On the tall, ancient, brown trees
The fresh, bright forest.

Jade Brumpton (12)
The Colne Community School, Brightlingsea

Snow - Haiku

It was a cold night
Snow laid on the ground, silent
White as a blanket.

Samuel King (12)
The Colne Community School, Brightlingsea

Hedgehog - Haiku

The hedgehog was dead
It had been edging along
To the giant kerb.

Zak Bush (12)
The Colne Community School, Brightlingsea

Haikus

Chirping as it cracked.
Fluffing up like a balloon.
Slowly cuddling up.

Fly like a big bird.
Squawking as it catches food.
Safely takes it home.

Megan Lamb (12)
The Colne Community School, Brightlingsea

Frosty And Jelly - Haikus

Frosty as ice cubes
Melting in the lovely sun
Trickling down the door

Jelly running down
Like a pile of squidgy gel
Running down the side.

Gemma Baker (12)
The Colne Community School, Brightlingsea

Dying

I'm lying in a bed in a cold, gloomy room
Struggling for a spark of life
Slowly, silently suffering
You don't see it but I know it
I'm slowing down like a car
At a traffic light
In a bed, in a room, in a hospital
Slowly but surely *dying*.

Bethany Nice (12)
The Colne Community School, Brightlingsea

Friendship

Friendship is a big gift
Sitting at your front door,
Boyfriends come and go
But friends will always be there,
Friendships can last for years
Or just for weeks,
Friends can make you laugh or sob
But the best thing about friendship
Is having
Friends!

Chloe Springall (13)
The Colne Community School, Brightlingsea

Piekus

Without it I die,
I look at you and just sigh,
Oh delicious *pie*.

I love you so much,
You brighten up my dull life,
Can't get enough *pie*.

Barney Graham (12)
The Colne Community School, Brightlingsea

Flowery Poem

Beautiful, colourful flowers,
Lively, silky petals,
It's shiny, sparkly and lovely.

Laura Penn (12)
The Colne Community School, Brightlingsea

Haikus

A Port
Stuck in the middle
Of a busy, crowded port
Waiting to travel

Stuck In Winter
Frozen icicles
Hang from all over my arms
While I am stuck here

Rolling All Over
Rolling all over
While I am trembling in fright
'Cause the storm roars here.

Rosie Roberts (12)
The Colne Community School, Brightlingsea

A Place Inside Myself

I finally escaped
From this haunted and taunted place
I'm so confused now.

The thing that waits for me
I just can't look now
It's taking control of me
Watching what I see.

Charlotte Sable (13)
The Colne Community School, Brightlingsea

My Last War

As the sound of the bullets deafen me
I ask myself
Why did this happen?
Why am I still here after seven years?

As I charge over to help the wounded
A bullet narrowly avoids me
I tell myself
I am going to get nowhere standing around in the trench

Doing nothing, I will have to go out there
And shoot as many enemies as I can see
But as I do that
A grenade blows me to pieces.

Nathan Kelly (14)
The Colne Community School, Brightlingsea

WWII

Machine guns rattling like keys in a tin!
People screaming like a newborn baby!
Blood flowing as fast as the sea!
When the fight is over, the ghosts that remain,
The bodies in the sea,
Waiting, waiting for the predators of the sea!

Sam Nunn (13)
The Colne Community School, Brightlingsea

Rain - Haiku

The rain hammered down
It poured through my burning soul
It tore me apart.

Gareth Hammond (13)
The Colne Community School, Brightlingsea

Hate

Hate is lightning coming from a cloud.
Hate is blood dripping off a knife.
Hate is a screaming shadow.
Hate is a shallow pool of blood.
Hate is a knife stabbing your heart.
Hate is your mind full of bad memories.
Hate is a lost soul.
Hate is a room full of jealousy.
Hate is your crying heart.
Hate is a shady corner.
Hate is war.
Hate is a sizzling fire.

Clare Wenman (13)
The Colne Community School, Brightlingsea

Is This The End?

Is this the end?
I saw it, it was huge;
Bigger than I could ever imagine.
Everyone just stood there watching it in shock.
People were on their roofs with tears running down their faces.
People trapped, people drowning.
It is the end, I know it,
I can feel it.

Kayleigh Wilkinson (12)
The Colne Community School, Brightlingsea

The Rose - Haiku

The rose scent was sweet
Far too delicate to touch
Holding all your love.

Emma Cutter
The Colne Community School, Brightlingsea

Autumn And Winter - Haikus

Autumn
Leaves are tumbling
Autumn is coming today
Branches are so bare.

Winter
Snowing all around
Christmas cheer is spreading far
All across the land.

James Kildea (13)
The Colne Community School, Brightlingsea

Winter Times - Haiku

As the snow settled,
The wind blew ever harder,
With the scent of fear!

Wilf Hall (13)
The Colne Community School, Brightlingsea

Untitled

No time to watch the world
Have no time to see me cry
People rushing by.

Jessica Pagram (13)
The Colne Community School, Brightlingsea

Untitled

A mysterious creature lying staring at me with his big yellow eyes
His camouflage is fantastic, his stealth is as sharp as the tip of
an axe
He moves slowly and quietly through the dark, eerie night
He sits outside the house screeching and screaming to the max

He hunts meat for his food, he crouches low, ready to leap on
his prey
When it's in his mouth, he swings it round waiting for it to die
His speed is incredible for killing creatures, he's as fast as a dart
He is everywhere and nowhere

The creature finds his nest in places that you would least expect
But I know where he sleeps - under a tree with a few bones of rat
I approach him slowly in the dead dawn of the morning and to
my surprise
The yellow eyes get closer and closer until I can see it's just
a stray cat.

Owen Culham (12)
The Deanes School, Benfleet

My Little Baby

She has love which gleams like a rainbow,
With a body thin and puny,
Amazing, alert fur that raves a friendly figure.

A comical nose tickle every now and then,
With whiskers long and sharp,
A delicate thing, affectionate.

My little baby,
My little baby,
A star.

Gemma Bollu (12)
The Deanes School, Benfleet

Untitled

This cat of mine
She was so lively
Icy was her name
Weird name wasn't it?

Icy was a weird one
Always here one moment
And gone the next
But she was a good cat
And always came back.

But then one day she left
I thought she could come back
Like before
A day had gone by
And no sign of her.

I was panicking
Looking in every direction
Down every road
Down every crack
I searched my house upside down
But I knew that she was gone.

Icy was her name
She used to live with me
But that was until it happened
And she left me
For good.

Katherine Turner (13) & Charlee Fitzpatrick (12)
The Deanes School, Benfleet

The Waves

In the winter the cliffs always fear
A giant, mystical monster
That's called the waves.

Smashing the cliffs
Tearing them down
The giant monster tears away.

Even when the summer comes
And the currents go away
The cliffs stay in fear
Of the monster called the waves.

Paul Moss (12)
The Deanes School, Benfleet

The Red Letter

She wished that this feeling would never end.
'I love you,' she said, but he pulled away.
'I'm leaving,' he hesitated, 'for the army.'
She gasped for breath as his words stabbed through her heart.
Her happiness slithered away; unbearable grief paralysed her body.
She did not hear his promises to write
And return home afterwards.

Four months had passed, no letter received.
Summer had ended, the deep autumn gloom reflecting her
empty soul.

Then it came.
The red letter through the letter box marked 'urgent'.
She collapsed on the floor.
Her mind swirled with the howls of pain;
She could taste the blood as she watched it slowly seep from
his body.

He said he would never leave her.
She wished this feeling would end.

Rebecca Jordan (14)
The King John School, Benfleet

The Way An Artist Works

An artist paints a glorious picture,
Of a glorious picture of an artist.
The blue of the seas, grey of the skies,
The choice of the colours on the palette.
Back and forth, back and forth,
Bold strokes, wispy strokes, all different techniques he could use.

Some criticise, some admire, or some even ignore the works of
an artist,
But the artist doesn't care what people think.
He has a passion for art, his passion inspired,
From what he sees, not what he knows.
The lake, he paints not a pure blue,
But a mix of murky green, brown and black.

The artist paints when he is in the mood,
The mood to open up his mind, his eyes, his artistic senses.
No matter what the weather,
If he's in the mood, he paints, sun, rain, sleet and snow,
Either from the comfort of his own home, or outside with nature.
If it's dark it doesn't matter, it will add to the picture, he says.

Becky Bromley (11)
The King John School, Benfleet

The Smell Of Wolf

Without Mum,
I kept crying,
The smell of wolf,
Kept me crying.
Nowadays I'm keeping fine,
But when Mum wasn't there,
Slower went the time.

Josh Hitchcock (14)
The King John School, Benfleet

A Bush's Tale

(With help from some bees)

At the front of our house,
There is a bush,
A very butterfly in its way.

In autumn it slumps,
(Boring in brown),
Its flowers all faded away.

In winter it turns,
As white as the snow,
While children play in the street.

Then in early spring . . .
It does nothing,
(Except maybe show a bit more green).

Then a miracle happens:
Slowly but surely,
The buds start to bloom,
First becoming greener,
Then larger,
And fuller
Until . . .

The bees appear to suckle the sweet nectar,
That now rests in the hearts of the purple petals,
That now race with each other to show the most colour.
Then another bee comes,
And another . . .
And another . . .
And another . . .
Until the bush is a purple buzz
(The butterfly in full glory returns).

Joy McManus (14)
The King John School, Benfleet

What If . . .

If I were God, there would be no hunger,
If I were God, everyone would have fun,
If I were God, there wouldn't be wars,
There would be no need for armies and guns.

If I were rich, I would have loads of money,
If I were rich, I would have a huge pool,
If I were rich, I would live in a mansion,
If I were rich, it would be so cool!

If I could have any job at all,
I'd be an actor or a vet,
If I were an actor I'd be in loads of films,
But if I wasn't, I'd look after pets.

I'd hate to be a girl because I'd have to wear dresses,
And if I was, I'd be perfect at school,
We'd all be sissy and all hold hands,
And I'd have to go and shop at the mall.

I think being different might not be so great.
I wouldn't want to be a responsible man.
I definitely wouldn't want to wear a frock.
I suppose I'm happy the way I am!

Dominic Coombs (11)
The King John School, Benfleet

Performing A Song (Gold Rush)

Stepping up,
Emotions changing,
Feeling tense,
Also exciting,
Scary time,
Curtains open,
Crowd ready to see,
What lies before them,
Breath of air,
Gold rush.

Alex Whybro (12)
The King John School, Benfleet

Mutation

I am but a lonely jellyfish
I was born this way
Next to a nuclear power plant
And it is here I will stay.

I am not a strong swimmer
For my legs are stumpy and short
I swim slightly to the left
And my gammy legs get caught.

The nuclear waste gave me three eyes
Other sea creatures don't understand
Sometimes they whip me with seaweed
While others pelt me with sand.

Other fish laugh and giggle
Some just turn away
Ever since I was little
No one wants to play.

Sometimes I swim near humans
Their bodies are as freaky as mine
I have many eyes like them
But they will always have a spine.

I hope to find a companion one day
Someone to share my sorrow
Some creature who will appreciate me
That day is always tomorrow.

I am but a lonely jellyfish
I was born this way
Next to a nuclear power plant
And it is here I will stay.

Jennifer Turner & Abigail Ponton (16)
The King John School, Benfleet

The Last Day Of School

It's the end of school
And everyone's happy.
All the children are chat, chat, chatty
On the last day of school.
Pencils and paper fly through the air
But even the teachers just don't care.
They just want the kids out of their hair
On the last day of school.

None of the children are paying attention,
They don't care, they won't get a detention
On the last day of school.
All the children want to forget,
But they will all remember
They have got to go back to school in September,
For their first day of school.

Amy Hadley (11)
The King John School, Benfleet

The Meadow

The sun is out,
The birds are singing,
On this beautiful day.

Cows are grazing,
Sheep are sleeping,
On the green grass.

A scarecrow in his uniform,
Scaring all the crows,
What a wonderful scene to see.

Sarah Parkes (14)
The King John School, Benfleet

Trigger

As I rise slowly from the bed,
Everything falls silent,
The target I want is straight ahead.
Time seems to freeze as we lock eyes,
Everything is at stand-still,
The look on his face could petrify.
My arm rises to reveal the decider,
He is the same I can see,
Staring at his face I see her.
My hand wrapped around at perfect aim,
Pulling it close to me,
I fire it off, feeling the pain.
Staring at the corpse is all I see,
The gun drops to the ground,
This is what the war has done to me.

Clare Raker (14)
The King John School, Benfleet

The Battle

There's a battle between two leaders in the west,
They have got to decide who really is the best,
In the north there are six girls dancing to a beat,
Complicated moves for their arms and small feet,
The south is where a feast fit for a king takes place,
Not a care for the mess on their hands and their face,
And a strategic game starts in the far east,
Who will be brave enough to hunt for the great beast?
Then the sound of the bell rings round,
I was just in the school playground.

Amie Gear (16)
The King John School, Benfleet

Friends And Family

Family is a God-given thing,
But friendship can be where it all begins.
Friends are with you forever,
Always through good and bad.
Families are always together,
Through happy and sad.
They get you through the day,
With some fun along the way.
It can be a difficult game . . .
Friends are people that you can choose,
But be careful that you don't lose.
There's nothing that they can't make you feel glad about,
They fill you with love and never doubt.
A family is something never to be neglected or forgotten,
Many things happen for a reason,
But this doesn't give you an excuse not to believe them.
That is where the saying comes from:
You can choose your friends,
But you have your family forever!

Samantha Toomer (14)
The King John School, Benfleet

The Scarlet Macaws

The red of their feathers is blood on a shirt,
Creeping away from the wound.
Then there is yellow contrasting the red,
Running to look for the moon.

Next there is blue, electric and bold,
Screaming out to you.
The highlight of green is barely seen,
But adds to the wondrous blue.

The last flick of red is light in the dark,
Without it the world would seem grey.
Though it flies away, it will leave its mark,
And return on a bright new day.

Rianne Lowe (13)
The King John School, Benfleet

The Third Company

The company started crawling across the ground,
As the light before them started to down,
They climbed the hill to the top,
Then they had to stop.
There stood a Nazi base,
Fear started to swell in their face.
They got their rifles and clawed along,
They had to take out the defences till they were all gone.
They shot the guards one by one,
And had to reload and make a run.
The team split up into four,
The guards, they knew, were all in a snore.
They all had their missions in their groups,
They had to go with a snoop.
They had to kill the captain of the base,
Then had to blow up the place.
The other two decided to work together,
To contact the base team called 'snake leather'.
They got to the captain's room,
They set some bombs to go boom.
They got the radio and sent a message,
To send a chopper to pick them up.
They got to the weapon store and planted the bomb,
Now it was time they were gone.
They got out into the chopper very quick,
Five men got airsick.
The base exploded into the air,
Like a firework display at a fair.
The mission was a big success,
That was their first mission and the best.

Brendan Young (12)
The King John School, Benfleet

Best Friends!

A best friend makes you smile,
Not just for a while,
They make you smile all day long,
And then you sing a song!

A best friend makes you laugh,
And they look daft,
They make life extremely fun,
And when you've stopped you look like the sun.

When you're down in the dumps,
You think of your enemies as lumps,
They are always there,
And they always care.

If you want to have a best friend,
Follow these guidelines,
And you will be as popular as
David Beckham.

Jessica Smith (12)
The King John School, Benfleet

Family And Co

My family means so much to me,
They always seem to be there,
But friends seem to come and go,
Why is life so unfair?

Molly was so different though,
Our love was a different love,
She was always there like Family and Co,
I loved her like a newborn dove.

But we were separated tragically,
War had taken over,
Maybe we'll be reunited magically,
Lucky, like a four-leaf clover.

Alexandra Butler (14)
The King John School, Benfleet

A Dark Night

Nervously, I lie awake,
Trembling with an unknown fear,
With the doors that creak and that eerie sound,
The sound that only I can hear.

Cautiously, I look around,
To watch if someone else is there,
Spine-chilling thoughts flow through my head,
As I bide the night and stay aware.

Alarming sounds, they bump and drip,
A shock to not know what they are,
The curtains blow and the floorboards creak,
And the moonlight glares from afar.

Those anonymous figures dancing,
To the sounds of the solitary tune,
When the silhouettes come out tonight,
And lurk in the corners from the light of the moon.

Is it just my imagination?
The bumps, the creaks of agitation,
Soon this sinister magic comes to an end,
Maybe just exaggeration?

Faye Watts (13)
The King John School, Benfleet

My Father

My father was a lumberjack,
But one day it all went wrong,
He saved a boy,
And lost his life,
Can we live on without him?
We just don't know.

Sam Courtenay (13)
The King John School, Benfleet

My Life

My mum says I was six weeks early,
Although tiny, a perfect girlie.

At five I started school,
I loved it, I thought it was cool.

Now I've started senior school,
I have fun playing netball.

For my dream job, of being an author,
It might earn me a dog, cuddly and soft.

I've a family now,
A husband and a daughter,
My brother has been slaughtered.

I'm lying in my chair,
Rested and quiet,
I still remember my first diet.

My days have ended now,
Hopefully I'll see you soon,
I lie rested and soothed,
Goodbye world, I've enjoyed my time with you.

Elizabeth Ellis (12)
The King John School, Benfleet

Beautiful, Blue Butterfly.

Often I walk down the quiet lane,
I hear the sound of the river flowing,
There are beautiful, blue butterflies,
Fluttering around the foxgloves,
And bees making buzzing sounds.
I like to watch the bees collecting pollen,
As I walk down the quiet lane,
I look up at the bright blue sky,
And watch the clouds float softly by.
I can picture my father up there,
High, high, high.

Ashia Soper (14)
The King John School, Benfleet

Unpeaceful

Stillness seemed to be about in the room after Father died,
I can still hear his voice, even now,
The smell of the pipe is here, but weaker,
His voice is vibrating in my head,
Crying, 'Tommo, Tommo!'
He told us he'll be here, but he lied!
It's all my fault that he died!
I'm physically disturbed by his death,
I am unhappy and I wish Father
Could come back to this Earth.

I can't tell anybody what happened,
If I do, peace will be broken,
Our names won't be the peaceful family anymore,
I've made it unpeaceful, for sure!
I wish Father could hear me now,
Saying sorry from the bottom of my heart.

Zaheda Khanum (14)
The King John School, Benfleet

Wartime!

Guns are shooting all around me,
Hurt men are shouting, 'Help me, please,'
Fires rage all over the city,
And smoke invades all surrounding seas.

Dead bodies lie not peaceful,
As disaster floats in the air,
Family lives have been turned upside down,
And happiness is found nowhere!

Laura Hemsworth (13)
The King John School, Benfleet

Love Is An Emotion

Confusion is a feeling caused by love,
Cupid, I think I need your help,
Send your arrows from above,
It's painful to see him,
It hurts to say,
That this emotion I'm feeling will not go away,
His voice is so gentle,
And he's always there you see,
There's got to be something there
Between him and me.
There's something about him,
He's special and sweet,
Whenever he's near, my heart skips a beat,
I wish I stood a chance,
Plus I think he likes me,
But that's beside the point,
He's way out of my league.

Amiee Wheeler (14)
The King John School, Benfleet

Loneliness

Loneliness is the boy that cries,
Loneliness is as small as a fly,
Loneliness has no heart or soul,
Loneliness is the emptiness of a hole,
Loneliness is an empty home,
Loneliness is when there's an awful groan,
Loneliness is sad when you need a home,
Loneliness is poor when under a bridge,
Loneliness is like an empty fridge,
Loneliness is a break in your heart,
Loneliness is as sharp as a dart,
Some of the pain will never heal,
And for evermore, the pain you'll feel.

James Compton (13)
The King John School, Benfleet

In The Morning Sun

Walks in the hedges,
Of meadowsweet names,
Roses I admire,
Red, pink, blue and yellow.

Flowers are here,
Flowers are there,
Here the bees come,
In the morning sun.

The honeysuckle's sweet,
The foxgloves are blooming,
We lie here quite settled,
All through the day.

Walks in the hedges,
Of meadowsweet names,
Roses I admire,
Red, pink, blue and yellow.

Hannah Calver (13)
The King John School, Benfleet

Butterflies

Butterflies
Spinning round and round gently
In the sky.

Glittering
To be free in the blue sky
In the sun.

Glistening
Wishing I could fly gently
Gracefully.

Rhyanna Matthews (11)
The King John School, Benfleet

Fly With The Angels

Look up to the sky,
The clouds float by,
Forever and always,
I'll be by your side,
Don't ever forget,
The memories we kept,
The laughs we had,
And the love we felt.
I'll never forget you,
I don't fly with the angels,
I'm with you
And once and once only.
I love you
And always have,
Forever and always,
The clouds float by.

Kelly MacKenzie (13)
The King John School, Benfleet

Forgive Me

I walked into the room
And everyone stopped talking.
My heart sank as she stared at me
And then she looked away.
I sat down on an empty chair
In the corner of the room.
Maybe tomorrow she'll forgive me,
Maybe one day.

Jess Andrews (13)
The King John School, Benfleet

The Apple Tree

There is an apple tree that I know which is a few minutes walk away.
It is in a field surrounded by a drystone wall.
Through different seasons of the year, different animals graze in
                                                        the field.
From the moment it wakes up after the cold, long winter,
                                its shoots start to grow again.
Butterflies and birds start to dance and twirl through the air
                                and round the tree they sing merrily.
They then disappear for another year until it is this time again.
When it starts to blossom in late spring, the blossom glides
                through the leaves into blossom men on the ground.
In the summer when it gives its apples, they turn golden,
And when they fall,
They are wrapped in a pink ribbon and net with a napkin below.
The rabbits run round and play games when it is autumn,
Which is the time the leaves fall to the ground,
And it gets ready to go back to sleep.

Alexander Foster (11)
The King John School, Benfleet

The Rainbow

Red   The colour of love and luck
Orange   The colour of the sun, gold and warmth
Yellow   The sign of happiness and wealth
Green   The sign of grass, fake or real, it's always there to last
Blue   The ocean all big and blue
Indigo   The colour of dreams, dream a better life
Violet   The colour of many flowers, pretty and bright.

Leah Scudder (12)
The King John School, Benfleet

Why?

What is the world coming to?
People dying all around,
Thinking about the whole world,
It's hard, it makes my head hurt,
It makes me feel sick inside.
The plane and the Twin Towers,
Why bother?
What was the point?
Thousands died and suffered pain,
It's appalling what we do,
And it is us doing it.
I think of different things,
But my brain cannot cope.
The things bad humans do,
Like the young five-year-old boy,
Why did they try to hang him?
And it was kids my age too.
That kid died because of them
Why bother?
What was the point?
What could a five-year-old do?
It's not fair, he was just five,
What is the world coming to?

Samantha Hyder (13)
The King John School, Benfleet

Love

Love is fair
And love is blind,
It's out of sight
And out of mind.
So why aren't you with me still,
Like hummingbird and daffodil?
Morning dew slips off the grass,
But now our love, it's here to last.

Sam Watts (12)
The King John School, Benfleet

Dragon Riders

Mysterious and dark
Flying through the night
Souls are connected
And eyes are bright.

Dragon from egg
And human from womb
Both live an eternity
Neither are doomed.

Though they are sworn
To a life of magic and fighting
For good and for justice
The dragon is biting.

For they fly like no other
For their life has no plan
They'll be together forever
The dragon and man!

Amy Beck (13)
The King John School, Benfleet

Space

I am black and white
And have been here forever.
Never moving,
Ever growing.
In this place,
All direction has gone,
Yet into the vacuum
I have gone.
Can you guess what I am?

Alexander Rosario (11)
The King John School, Benfleet

The Sight Of A Horse

There I was standing on the shore,
Listening to the waves crash and roar,
Round the corner I could see,
Pure white Snowey came to me.

She ran past me like a bird in the sky,
She was so beautiful, I was going to cry,
Her mane and tail shone so bright,
She ran away at the speed of light.

There I was standing on the shore,
Just listening to the waves crash and roar,
Is it possible for me to see,
Pure white Snowey free as can be?

Phillip Shepherd (13)
The King John School, Benfleet

I Wish

I wish to land on the sun one day,
I wish I could chase all the birds away.
I wish to have a flash car,
I wish to be a movie star.

I wish to travel the whole wide world,
I wish to see my idol's hair being curled.
I wish I was loved by someone,
But never be known as no one.

I wish I had all these wonderful things,
But for now they're all just dreams.
If I had one main wish, it would be to never die,
So I won't have to say goodbye!

Kayleigh Game (12) & Chloe Green (13)
The King John School, Benfleet

Love

Love is just a word,
It has no meaning.
To others it does,
But to many, it's a feeling.
Love is all around you,
You will find it soon,
Maybe under the stars,
Or over the moon.
It's a romantic walk on the beach,
Love is something you can't teach.
It's found deep inside you,
That only love can bind
Two.

Yazmin Aworer (13)
The King John School, Benfleet

The Sun

The sun is a big ball of light.
The sun never glows at night.
It shines all day,
Then hides away.
When it comes up,
It's a brand new day.
When I'm about,
The sun is out.
It cheers me up
And makes me shout,
And it makes me run about.
The sun is a golden ring.

Paige Brown (12)
The King John School, Benfleet

Animals

Animals are running around,
It's nice to hear the sound.
Monkey and cats,
Pigs and bats.
Animals are everywhere,
Even over there.
Animals are being born,
In the night and in the dawn.
Rabbits and frogs,
Always hopping along logs.
Trees have snakes,
Fish live in lakes,
Animals are everywhere.

Callum Weir (12)
The King John School, Benfleet

The Sun

The sun is a star,
Like an oven with nothing to control it.
The sun is a ball of fire.
The sun is a child's ray,
When they've lost their way,
Like a candle in the night.
The sun is like a shooting star,
Travels to different countries,
Near and far.
It goes away at night,
When it comes up,
The world is filled with light.

Leanne Cahill (13)
The King John School, Benfleet

The Sea

Blue and green are the colours,
It sparkles and shines in the sun.
Lots of creatures live under it,
Playing and having fun.
Sea horses, squid and fish,
All are one big family.
But the sea is very deep,
So you won't be able to see.
The sea also carries transport,
Like roads, tracks and even the air,
It does make a lot of noise,
Growling like a bear.
If it is quite dark,
Don't go near the edge,
Because you might not be able to see,
The end of the ledge.
This is just a warning,
So don't be scared off,
The sea is quite playful,
Just don't catch a cough.

Chloe Thomas (11)
The King John School, Benfleet

School

School is like a prison
It never gets better
The walls are damp
And the floor's even wetter.

The lessons are boring
Trying to get sleep
The students are snoring
Each day of the week.

Vincent Mudd & Sean McKinlay (12)
The King John School, Benfleet

Untitled

Hear the rain, the pouring rain
Pattering down without a name
Hear the wind blowing, what a shame
Falling down, all the same.

I stand there freezing
Looking round
The wind still wheezing
Sky to ground.

Looking for something
Looking for someone
But I can't see them
But I can hear them trembling.

You're there somewhere
I can hear you thinking
Out there somewhere
Your great mind ticking.

Hannah Horn (12)
The King John School, Benfleet

The Past And The Present

The past and the present are quite strange things,
Bad things happen,
Good things happen,
We really don't think what happens, happens.
So what do people do about it?
They put things right, but make things worse.
Nobody knows, nobody knows,
Everything is different to what we think now.
The weather and friends just go by,
We grow day by day, but we don't think why.
The past and the present are quite strange things.

Lauren Penny (11)
The King John School, Benfleet

Help Me!

Hi, I'm Ben,
I lived with my mum,
It used to be fun,
But something changed.

I loved my mum,
Well, most of the time,
But she smacked me
And that's not all.

I got bruised,
I got scared,
I got abused,
Please help me.

She got a knife,
Now I can't see,
She changed my life,
She hated me.

I got bruised,
I got scared,
I got abused,
Please help me.

I wanted to live,
Get married, have kids,
A home of my own
And someone to love.

But I got bruised,
I got scared,
Got abused,
I hate my mum!

Penny Mathers (12)
The King John School, Benfleet

Dinosaurs

Dinosaurs, there were many of them,
Not 30, not 50, not 210,
Oh, there was:

D iplodocus
I guanodon
N anosaurus
O viraptor
S inosauropteryx
A llosaurus
U tahraptor
R hamphorhynchus
S tegosaurus
and the rest

B ut everyone knows they're stone-dead,
O nly fossils are there with naught in their head,
Y es, everyone knows they're dead,
in other words, *extinct!*

Alex Marsh (11)
The King John School, Benfleet

Soft Little Teddy Bear

Soft little teddy bear on my bed,
Soft little teddy bear rests his head.
Soft little teddy bear helps me sleep,
Soft little teddy bear doesn't make a peep.

Luke Goringe (11)
The King John School, Benfleet

The Jungle

Deep, dark and spooky,
Trees as tall as skyscrapers,
No light filtering through.
Grass as still as death,
No breeze whispering through,
Breath as hot as the desert,
No air trickling through.
Birds silent in the trees,
No sound echoing through.

What stirs in the jungle?
What slithers through the trees?
What creeps through the grass?
Nobody sees . . .
Until that last moment,
There's death on the breeze.

Keiran Record (11)
The King John School, Benfleet

Me And My Friends

Me and my friends
Sasha, Laura and Ben
Walking down the street
Stepping all in beat
We all enjoy the same hobbies
Like riding our bikes
Great minds think alike.

Me and my friends
Sasha, Laura and Ben
Walking in the park
Hearing the dogs bark
We were all swinging on the swing really high
Touching the sky
Great minds think alike.

Rosa Frankis (11)
The King John School, Benfleet

War

War, war, what a waste of time,
It can kill loads of lives,
Including mine.
If we could all get along,
That would be great,
But it doesn't look that way,
Not at this rate.
I don't know if I shall survive,
I don't want to die,
I want to be alive.
I'm so tired,
I'm so scared,
The people attacking,
I wish they cared.
I can't describe how I feel,
I can't believe this is all real.
All these horrible noises and smells,
I can hear crying from all the boys and girls.
All these people shouting and screaming,
I never again want to have this feeling.
People I love are not here anymore,
Shall I live?
I'm not sure.

Lauren Selway (12)
The King John School, Benfleet

A Great Mind

A mind of a child,
Free and wild,
What will it create?
Maybe a dragon,
Or a colourful wagon,
Or even a planet called Pop!
It will create such magical things.
A mind of a child,
Free and wild,
What will it create?
A magical land from far, far away,
Where only the quietest thing may stay.
Maybe a tree full of sweets,
Or maybe a tree full of magical treats,
Or maybe a stairway that never ends,
Or just a made up, imaginary friend.
The mind of a child,
Free and wild.

Daniel Fielding Smith (12)
The King John School, Benfleet

Be Yourself

Why wish upon a star?
Why not stay who you are?
If you're big, if you're small,
It doesn't matter, just stay cool.

If you're picked on, don't be sad,
They are jealous of what you have.
The inside matters, not the out,
That's all you have to think about.

Or tell someone about your thoughts,
They'll help you out, the bully will be caught.
Whatever you do, just have faith,
Your friends and family will keep you safe.

Courtney Dye (12)
The King John School, Benfleet

Transformation

Beating hearts
Missing chances
Secret smiles
Stolen glances.

Could you ever whisper the words
That I would love to hear?
I live to listen for those words
I would die to feel you near.

This bittersweet torture has transformed my numb senses
They are now alive and dancing.
But fading away at your cruelty
This painful lust is everlasting.

Beating hearts
Missing chances
Secret smiles
Stolen glances.

Emily Blake & Rebecca Jackson (15)
The King John School, Benfleet

Stars

Quiet in the silent night,
Shining down their rays of light.
They leave us in the early morning,
But again we see them when day is dawning.
They show us signs and interest us,
But to see how beautiful they are is a must.
Like fireflies sticking to the sky,
We ask ourselves why?

What are they?
Stars.

Laura Norris (11)
The King John School, Benfleet

All Alone

Every morning I wake up with the same feeling,
My stomach reeling,
Sweat dripping off my face on the way,
Legs buckling as I walk through the gate.
I look down at the floor as I turn the corner,
My head is drooped like a heavy mourner,
I hear their laughs like a hyena's call,
They're hanging over me, so very tall.
Shouting at me and calling me names,
Snarling at me, saying I'm lame,
I try to forget that I'm a small, little coward,
I try and think I'm full of power.
But it doesn't work when you're now on the floor,
Being beaten and laughed at to the core,
I'm left all alone now, battered with kicks,
My eyes start filling, pricking like pricks.
They've stolen my things and my silver chain,
I know tomorrow it will happen again,
I wish I was different, pretty and cool,
I want to be the best, best in school.
I lie there, waiting for someone to come,
I'm really cold, my body is numb,
I don't like school, I want to go home!
But nobody's around, I'm all alone.

Charlotte Weathersbee (12)
The King John School, Benfleet

Under The Bed

Every night when I go to bed
I hate to turn the light out
Because I know what is under the bed.

Under the bed is an endless pit,
Under the bed where it's never lit,
Under the bed where it's cold, dark and scary,
Under the bed where the monsters are hairy.

I sit awake
For hours and hours
So nothing can jump out on me.

Under the bed there's an old lady called Mary,
She may be a fairy, but she's really quite scary,
Under the bed where the bogeyman lies,
Under the bed where the dragon still flies.

I finally fall asleep
To their content -
But I still have dreams about it.

Under the bed it's as plain as the skies,
Though it's also the place where the demon lies,
Under the bed live the living dead,
Under the bed is a place filled with *dread.*

Tom Berry (11)
The King John School, Benfleet

The Thing

It rambled ranting towards me
Its tail thumping threateningly, thrashing behind
It leapt loathingly, lashing like a lion lord
Landing loudly lengthways, leering at its prey - me.

I heard its giant footsteps coming from behind
I saw its giant claws like shining razor blades
I felt its fur all coarse and prickly, rubbing on my arms
I smelt its venomous, vile, garlic breath when it grew closer
Its teeth were giant lumps of steel slashing down to get me.

Suddenly
I heard thunder
Crashing crazily
Through the sky
Sharp
Short
Shots
Of lightning . . .

Ellen Stratton (12)
The King John School, Benfleet

Useless

She's as useless
As a shop with no till
As a window with no sill
She's as useless
As a hand with no thumb
As a girl with no bum

She's as useless
As a school with no chair
As a country with no mayor
She's as useless
As a computer with no mouse
As a girl with no house

She's as useless
As a car with no wheels
As an orange with no peel
She's as useless
As a pen with no ink
As a lip with no pink

She's as useless
As a girl with no hair
As a forest with no bear
She's as useless
As a boy with no nose
As a lady with no rose.

Jade Hardy (12)
The Sweyne Park School, Rayleigh

Cake

I don't like cooking
I'm not that good
To be good at cooking
You have to be good at listening
To be good at listening
You have to be good at cooking
And I will never be good at cooking or listening!

My sister is on a mission
To make the world's tallest cake
I don't think she will make it
But she is having fun with her mate

My brother's one of those boys
Who wants to do a fraction
He's pestering them so much
To let him be part of the action.

As for me
I'll try very hard
I'm the most artistic
And I'll help them create a card.

All this is in aid of the NCH
The National Children's Homes
They're to bring less lucky children to safety
So that they are not alone.

Alexandra Tyson (12)
The Sweyne Park School, Rayleigh

Cheesecake!

Made out of savoury,
But tastes so sweet,
I really love cheesecake,
Oh, what a treat!

The filling is creamy,
The base is a delight,
This cheesecake is dreamy,
Hooked after one bite!

Fluffy and yellow,
Round and yummy,
So grab a fork
And straight to your tummy!

So soft and cheesy,
I could eat it all day,
I'd get really fat,
But I'll eat it anyway!

This cake is delicious,
You know you can't resist,
So when Mum's shopping,
It's first on the list!

Lucy Barnes (14)
Thomas Alleyne School, Stevenage

Love

It is like a disease,
There is no cure,
You can't ignore it,
It's always there,
Resting in your heart,
It pulses around your body,
Makes you feel tingly inside,
It will come out at any time,
So don't be surprised when someone says,
'You've gone all shy, why are you blushing?'
This is how it works,
It's unpredictable.

When you're in love,
Your emotions could go up or down,
One minute you're happy,
The next you're sad,
You may find you can't stop thinking,
About this person you love,
You may seem lost without him,
Don't let it control your life.

Remember, love doesn't last forever,
So keep your friends first,
You may just find yourself alone,
If you let love control your life.

Chloe Williams (14)
Thomas Alleyne School, Stevenage

Forever

Every story is different
Each has their tale to tell
From the fairies to the witches
Their parts are played out well.
Every story takes you somewhere
It's different every time
Sometimes you can see it
The mountains you can climb.
The words are the footprints
On the snowy page
Wandering to nowhere
Held within their cage.
Every chapter holds suspense
It has a lesson to teach
Trying to win the battle
Though it feels just out of reach.
But when the tale's over
You go back to the start
But the stories are forever
They are always in your heart.

Domonique Curaba (14)
Thomas Alleyne School, Stevenage

The Forgotten Moments

Forgotten moments,
Those blank patches in your memory,
That make up most of your life,
The ones you forget straightaway.

A lingering glance at someone else on the train,
Items you stare at through a shop's windowpane,
Every cough, every laugh, every face that's new,
Every trivial article that appears on the news.

The sorrys the thank yous, the mumbled appeals,
For silence or movement, the pain we all feel,
From momentary mishaps and slow reactions,
The things that you pass, life's short distractions.

Things we never remember, that pass straight through our minds,
The parts of our life that we leave behind,
All of those times lost somewhere and somehow,
Life's forgotten moments that all add up to now.

Tessa Pope (14)
Thomas Alleyne School, Stevenage

Time

Every day the clock keeps on ticking,
And the light is devoured by the darkness.
When will we learn that you can't live forever?
You just have to wait and see.
If there's no one around,
But the ink keeps running black,
Will it still turn blue?
Will it still be true?
If we forget all of this,
Will life just carry on?
Will the clock keep ticking,
Even when we're gone?

Gemma Albone (13)
Thomas Alleyne School, Stevenage

Hunger

Hunger is as black as a shadow hanging over you
Like a never-ending scream whistling in the wind
Hunger deafens the air around you until you burst
And realise poverty is about to begin.

Hunger causes poverty all around, in every country
It's just whether you notice or ignore the mighty shout
Of a mother or a brother crying out for help
Until all the other people see that hunger is about.

Hunger through the night and hunger through the day
The echoing never stops flowing through the afraid
To ask for help, family, friends or someone else
But it hits you when you know what hunger has made.

The animal who goes through bins at night through hunger
The person who once knew no hunger, just food
The scavenger you've become can't be explained by words
The person you never thought you'd become, that's you!

Carys Page (14)
Thomas Alleyne School, Stevenage

My First Day

Looking around on my first day at school
Looking for new friends to meet
We could be so very cool
On my first day of school

Looking around at faces I do not know
I do not know which way to go
Up the stairs, left or right
I don't want to get into a fight

The first day of school has come to an end
I think I know who are my friends
I may be wrong, I may be right
You can't tell overnight.

Kirsty Turner (14)
Thomas Alleyne School, Stevenage

Here We Go

Here we go
We're off to war
Here we go
The reason we went
We do not know.
In the trenches two by two,
What came next?
We never knew.

So here we lie,
In a grave,
For not many men were saved.
We died for your country
Others died too
Don't forget
We died for you.

Kayleigh Henley (14)
Thomas Alleyne School, Stevenage

Loneliness

Loneliness is like being in a plastic ball,
Cut off from the world,
White, white as the clouds on a sunny day,
The buzz of a TV screen turning on.

Nothing, nothing else to hear,
Except the wind.

Loneliness looks like a desert,
Beyond the horizon,
Grey, grey like the fur on a wolf's back,
Anything more to smell, to hear, to feel.

Nothing, nothing else to hear,
Except the wind.

Loneliness, loneliness is sitting in a room on your own,
With the wind bashing your face.

Oliver Wisker (14)
Thomas Alleyne School, Stevenage

The Dentist

The trip I dread,
To the man I hate.
He scares me to death,
Even thinking about him.
His tight rubber gloves,
Inserted in my mouth,
Make me choke,
Until my eyes burst with tears.

Why do I need a check-up?
My teeth are really fine.
I clean them twice a day,
So why do they care?
They're not yellow,
Not brown or even wonky,
Perfectly straight and pearly white.

So why do I need to go to the dentist?
It's really a waste of time.
I'm about to go in,
Sweating and fearing.
I see him and,
Oh,
He looks okay.
Not scary or angry, but very calm,
Maybe it's okay after all.

Daniel Wilde (14)
Thomas Alleyne School, Stevenage

Teachers

Teachers are so boring
They are so annoying
Why do they keep picking on me?
I'm not a teacher's pet
So get it outta your head
What's two plus two?
I ain't got a clue!

They are meant to teach
But all they do is preach
About tucking in your shirt
Or the length of your skirt.

To be honest no one cares
About the style of your hair
Teachers just wanna embarrass you
But then again, what's new?

Teachers are so boring
They are so annoying
Why do they keep picking on me?
I'm not a teacher's pet
So get it outta your head
What's two plus two?
I ain't got a clue!

Georgina Oakley (14)
Thomas Alleyne School, Stevenage

Darkness

Darkness is black
And dark like depression,
It sounds as empty
And silent as space.

It has the stench
Of an abandoned dungeon,
And is empty and lonely
Like nothingness.

It feels like the woods
On a dark, moonless night,
Where things can't be seen
And it suffocates.

It closes in on you,
It wraps around you.
Nothing is there,
You're all on your own.

Your sight has been taken
By an invisible thief,
There's nowhere to go,
You can't escape.

In darkness you don't know
What could happen.
Nothing can be seen,
Just black!

Rachel Hodson (14)
Thomas Alleyne School, Stevenage

Cravings

Cravings are dark,
Like a splash of black ink,
They sound like teeth mauling a bone,
They smell rotten or bitter,
Like a body left for dead.

Cravings can manipulate,
Control your body,
They are parasites on your mind.
They are a pair of jaws that slowly eat you away,
Until you can resist them no longer,
And you give in to the temptations of the world.

Then becoming normal again,
Until the jaws of cravings
Come back to consume you
Once more.

Ross Selwood (14)
Thomas Alleyne School, Stevenage